W9-BLK-415

Writing Cookbooks

Judith Comfort

Self-Counsel Press
(a division of)
International Self-Counsel Press Ltd.

Copyright © 1997 by Judith Comfort.

All rights reserved.

No part of this book may be reproduced or transmitted in any form by any means — graphic, electronic, or mechanical — without permission in writing from the publisher, except by a reviewer who may quote brief passages in a review.

Printed in Canada

First edition: September 1997

Canadian Cataloguing in Publication Data

Comfort, Judith.
Writing cookbooks

(Self-counsel series)
ISBN 1-55180-115-9

1. Cookery — Authorship. I. Title. II. Series.
TX644.C65 1997   808'.066641   C97-910708-3

Self-Counsel Press
(a division of)
International Self-Counsel Press Ltd.

1704 N. State Street   1481 Charlotte Road
Bellingham, WA 98225   North Vancouver, BC V7J 1H1
U.S.A.   Canada

Contents

Introduction

If there's one message I'd like to communicate to anyone reading this book it is, "YOU CAN DO IT." Writers are not an exclusive group. Some would argue that this assortment of individuals has only one thing in common. Each one has broken through the mystique known as publishing. Each one has taken pure thought and transformed it into the printed page.

How did they do it? Everyone has his or her own story to tell, but it usually involves a combination of part luck, part timing, and a lot of hard work and commitment to see a project through to the bitter (or sweet) end. Getting into print is not for the easily discouraged. You have to really want to do it. You must be prepared to sell your ideas again and again, first to a publisher, then to the public, and occasionally to yourself in moments of doubt.

My own entry onto the printed page was a serendipitous one. It began when I acted on a vague feeling and carved out a private time for myself. Before my family woke up, in the cool early summer mornings, I would get up, gaze out at the harbor, sip freshly brewed coffee, and write. For me, the remarkable thing about writing has always been the surprise of what appears on the page. Observing the brain's ability to integrate seemingly disparate thoughts is still the biggest thrill of the writing process for me.

What came out in those first scratchings were memories of my grandmother's kitchen. I can't find those first attempts at writing. I never did submit or sell those particular words, but that same inspiration rose to the surface of my consciousness and spilled into print again and again. A few years later I wrote a back-page personal piece for *Canadian Living* magazine. The theme was the amount of time my grandmother spent in her kitchen (all day), in contrast to my mother (1950s housewife, chocolate chip cookies just out of the oven) and myself (modern, exhausted owner of 100 cookbooks who spent 20 minutes a day in the kitchen and barely had the strength to throw peanut butter sandwiches at the kids).

Years later, thoughts and ideas arising from those first few attempts influenced my approach to interviewing generations of the Puxley/Titus family for my book *Judith Comfort's Christmas Cookbook*.

The big event for me was to reach a point of confidence where I could show my writing to another soul. I finally shared it with my friend Steven Slipp, a graphic designer who had worked closely with a regional Maritime publisher. We agreed to submit ten book package ideas to the publisher. The company liked the one where I would travel the province of Nova Scotia, interviewing owners of country restaurants and inns to find out their culinary secrets.

I learned how to interview by interviewing. I learned how to test recipes by bringing home recipes and trying them out on my family and friends. I learned how to write — and I cannot emphasize this enough — by writing.

Steven came up with the brilliant title *Some Good*, which are the words that spring to Maritimers' lips when something is really delicious. Our book filled a niche, became a best-seller (many expatriate Maritimers bought it on the strength of the title alone!), and my writing career was launched. I have since written four more cookbooks and two travel guides, published dozens of magazine articles, and started to teach writing to adults and children. All this evolved out of a vague inkling, a desire to write "something," anything. The thrill for me continues to be, as it has always been, the process.

If I can do it, so can you. But be realistic about where you are. What do you need to do to reach your point of confidence? Do you need more practice in writing? Find a teacher in an evening class or a mentor you can trust. Get your stuff in print wherever you can, whether in a company newsletter or local paper. Give your writing away to whoever will give you a byline. Collect those clippings. They will be invaluable later when you submit your book proposal.

There is a lot of help out there in books. Writers like to write about writing. Check the shelves of the public library and you'll not only find books on how to write books and how to write a book proposal to submit to a publisher, but will also discover information about the publishers themselves: who they are and what they want. There are even books that tell you how to build up your confidence as a writer.

Want to go out on your own? Find a book on how to self-publish, set up a small business around your book, and promote it, too.

The chasm between the unpublished and the published is not as wide as you think, but as with any business venture, you have to do your homework. Thoroughly research your subject matter and your market, and assess the competition. Learn the discipline of technical writing and testing to guarantee a product with integrity. And, of course, be the best writer you can possibly be.

Some people with little ability are able to write a cookbook. A publisher may take you on if you are a celebrity whose name will guarantee sales. It's simple enough if there's enough money to hire editors and recipe testers to do most of the work. However, most of us will write our book ourselves. I highly recommend William Zinsser's book *On Writing*, which has been an inspiration to thousands of would-be writers.

I would also like to thank the following people for their advice and support: Anna Comfort, Alan Comfort, Cynthia Berney, Rachel Meier, Robert Kardolus, Jackie Ehlert, Wayne Decle, and Elizabeth Rains.

Wishing you the best of luck in bringing your book to life.

JUDITH COMFORT

xi

PART I
The Ingredients

1
A cookbook begins with an idea

a. Generating cookbook ideas

It's your idea, and it's a terrific idea. But will it sell? Publishing is like any business — there's an element of risk. No one really knows whether an idea is a good one until it is out there for the testing (and tasting).

If you believe in your idea, pursue it. Publishers are looking for writers who have the experience, passion, and tenacity to see their cookbook through to its publication. It's simple from the publishers' point of view — they want books that sell really well. But what is considered "really well" differs radically from national mainstream publishers to small regional presses, from large corporate-style publishers to basement-room hobbyists.

To find a home for your cookbook you need to find out where your book fits into the market of publishers but more importantly, you need to find out where your book fits into the market of cookbook buyers. Will it interest a few of your neighbors or is it an earthshaking concept with universal appeal? Is there a genuine need for it — is it a subject just asking to be written for a niche market anxious for the information? What are your personal priorities? Would you be happy with a small production run and an inexpensive, unillustrated, photocopied text? Or do you envision a glossy coffee-table volume? And is this vision consistent with your cookbook concept? Once you've answered these questions, you'll have an idea of which publisher might be right for you.

You can also, of course, choose to go the self-publishing route. For some cookbooks, community fund-raisers for example, this route is the more common one. Both will be discussed later in the book.

1. Are there any new cookbook ideas?

Good ideas for cookbooks arise out of the same fertile ground as good ideas for any book — the creative mind of a person with a passionate interest in the topic, someone who has conducted thorough research and thoughtfully considered readers' needs and interests.

Ideally you want to write a book on a topic that is new, so the book is really needed. For example, the vegetarian cookbooks that appeared in the early 1970s on the cusp of a revolutionary change in North American eating habits reflected readers' new interests. Everyone was hungry for a healthier lifestyle and the cookbooks that would help them create it.

So what's new? What's in? What are the trends in cookbook publishing and consumer eating habits? There are new food fashions emerging every day. Think about gearing your cookbook to these new trends. Talk to your local health food store about the latest in new foods, preparation methods, and cooking.

Because they have a shorter lead time than books, magazines are often the first place where information on new subjects or food trends is published. A good way to peruse subjects covered by many magazines is to browse through magazine indexes. These list the "hot" subjects you may not have seen in print before; take a look at *Reader's Guide to Periodical Literature* and the *Canadian Periodical Index*.

Remember to think about demographics when you are working on your cookbook concept. Population trends such as the number of people moving into retirement can have a dramatic impact on the type of cookbook that will be popular. Of course, demographics shouldn't be the only thing you bear in mind when planning your project, but it's a good idea to think of it as a factor when you are making those early decisions.

2. Types of cookbooks

There are thousands of cookbook titles in the marketplace. Hundreds of new ones are published every year. But there are far fewer categories of subject matter. Some books are combinations of a few concepts, for example, a community fund-raiser book of desserts. Here are some topics to start you thinking about a new, fresh idea.

(a) General

The general category of cookbook includes the old classics such as *Joy of Cooking* and *Fanny Farmer*. These are encyclopedic collections with a standard table of contents and expected chapters on everything from soups and appetizers to vegetables, meat, fish, and desserts.

(b) Community

Community cookbooks are cooperative amateur efforts (by, for example, church groups, museum societies, and cultural groups), usually written with fund-raising as a main objective. There are often many contributors, resulting in an uneven style, untested recipes, and varying quality. Many of these cookbooks, even from different parts of the continent, have similar recipes.

This being said, community cookbooks often capture local flavor, and some are gems. They preserve genuine regional treasures. Older ones captured cultural history that may otherwise have been lost.

Because community cookbooks are managed, written, and produced differently from other cookbooks, the next chapter is devoted to a discussion of community cookbooks. It also offers more ideas on topics for this type of cookbook.

(c) Culinary expert authors

Who better to write a cookbook than a professional chef or restaurateur? Cookbooks written by culinary experts can be either brilliant treatises or public relations tools to promote the eating establishment or career of the author. Cooking show hosts often write books as natural spin-offs to their shows and sell copies by mail order. Sales are practically guaranteed.

(d) Celebrity cookbooks

Write a celebrity cookbook if you are famous for any reason at all, or if you are related to someone famous, or if you cook for someone famous. For example, Regis and Kathy Lee wrote a cookbook. So did

Types of cookbooks:

- General
- Community
- Culinary expert author
- Celebrity
- Single ingredient
- Seasonal/holiday
- New technology
- Regional/ethnic
- Health/medical
- Lifestyle
- Cooking method
- Menu/meal
- Theme crossovers
- Miscellaneous original concept

5

David Letterman's mother, the King of Kensington's wife, and Oprah Winfrey's chef.

(e) Single ingredient

Single ingredient cookbooks that focus on one main food item, including such varied subjects as potatoes, salmon, and tofu, are hugely successful, probably because of the gift market for cookbooks. With changing food fashions and consumer expectations for the new and exciting, new products are being imported and produced every day, creating lots of opportunity for such cookbooks.

(f) Seasonal / holiday

Many collections of summer recipes, winter recipes, and Christmas recipes have been written. Consult a UNICEF calendar for a plethora of international holidays to be exploited for their culinary possibilities.

(g) New technology

First comes the kitchen gadget, next comes the cookbook. Consider the shelf life of the chafing dish cookbook, the fondue dish cookbook, and the deep fat fryer cookbook (definitely out of fashion with fat-conscious consumers now). Others include blender, food processor, clay baker, wok, microwave oven, and breadmaker cookbooks. Ask yourself, What machines are on the horizon?

(h) Regional / ethnic

With the homogenization of culture it has become a challenge to create a cookbook based on a regional theme (cooking of the American Midwest, for example). Ethnic cooking is also regional, for example, Russian cookery.

(i) Health / medical

Health/medical cookbooks dispense nutritional or medical advice along with the recipes. Examples include books for people with heart disease or diabetes.

(j) Lifestyle

Consumer eating habits have changed drastically in the last ten years because of health concerns and the influence of other cultures. Lifestyle cookbooks address eating in a holistic way. Vegetarian cooking is one example of lifestyle cooking.

(k) Cooking method

Cooking method cookbooks are written for readers who are not content with the overview offered by general encyclopedic cookbooks. These readers are looking for more detailed descriptions of cooking techniques and a disciplined attitude from culinary experts such as bakers. Books on baking, barbecuing, and preserving are examples of this type of cookbook.

(l) Menu / meal

Some cookbooks offer suggestions on what goes with what, but menu/meal cookbooks offer readers much more: recipes for a whole dinner party and instructions on how to do everything from sending invitations to folding napkins. Often focusing on entertainment or special events, these books may also be centered on more practical themes, such as family dinners in 30 minutes.

(m) Theme crossovers

Theme crossover cookbooks are half cookbook, half something else, for example, a mix of cooking and gardening, biography, or poetry.

(n) Miscellaneous original concept

Miscellaneous original concept cookbooks are the once-a-decade books that we all hope to write, the books that meet a genuine public need and provide information that doesn't exist in print anywhere else. Examples of this type of cookbook include *Better than Store Bought, Diet for a Small Planet*, and *Moosewood Cookbook*.

(o) Some silly and not-so-silly cookbook ideas

- Beautiful food as art cookbook
- When in North Dakota, cook as the North Dakotans do
- Famous quotes cookery
- Cooking on the right side of the brain
- Too-many-cooks cooking
- Entertaining for recluses
- Transcendental vegetation
- Kids' cool cookbook
- Famous headlines cookbook
- Best of Boston Bar
- Indulgent cooking for the stressed
- Wild greens cookery

- Great fish chefs share their secrets
- Molasses and maple syrup: pure ambrosia cooking
- Single dads and moms survival cookbook
- Intellectual fare
- Memories of a Ukrainian baba
- You don't have to be a chef
- Stewardship cooking
- Seasonal look at California
- Gadgetless cooking
- Cater your own party
- Flambé without fear
- Food survival
- Bland is fine
- Cooking for Fido
- Picky eaters' cookbook
- Sustainable planet eating
- Recipes from famous novels
- Dandelion cookery
- Eat the trees
- Peanut butter and other nuts
- Weird ingredient cooking
- Canoe camping delights
- Ten-minute dinners

3. Developing an idea

To develop a concept for your cookbook, start with an idea, even a fragment of a thought. Write it down. Many writers keep notebooks handy all the time, ready to jot down story or book ideas as they occur.

Let's say you have made an observation about the modern family's eating habits: no one seems to have time to sit down for a meal together. You wonder how people are coping. Who is doing the cooking and shopping? Are children getting the proper nutrition? How can your book help?

You talk to friends and acquaintances who offer a number of solutions. One mother cooks a complete meal and puts it on plates in the refrigerator to be microwaved later, after the hockey game, the ballet lesson, or the board meeting. In other families, parents and children takes turns cooking. Another person you interview prepares huge batches of sauces on the weekend, freezes them, and then re-heats as needed during the hectic week.

Can you create a cookbook concept from your observations and preliminary research? Ideas start to come to you: Teens Who Cook Dinner. Family Potlucks: Everyone Pitches In. The Reheat, Rehash Cookbook.

Sounds unappetizing, but you head to the library to look for recipes using leftovers that actually improve with age. You find soups and stews. And, wow! Yesterday's leftover stew is today's dumpling filling. The discussion in chapter 7 on researching your subject will help you understand methods of research and the various sources of information.

Many ideas are born from the question, "Who would you like to write for?" Determining your desired readership may help you generate a cookbook concept. But be careful: make sure you are up to the task. We would all like to think that famous chefs and owners of four-star restaurants would find our cookbook invaluable. Be realistic and success will be waiting just around the corner for you.

4. Write from experience

If you still don't have a specific idea for a cookbook, start with yourself. What makes you special? This is no time to be humble, just honest. You need to come up with ideas that someone else wants to buy. These ideas often come from things that you already know and do and care about. For example, if you grew up on a farm and had a garden, you likely have a good knowledge base on which to start your research into a fresh herb cookbook. Think about your ethnic background, whether it's Chinese, Mediterranean, Scottish, or a mixture. Did growing up in that culture give you insight into the cookery of your ancestors that would be of interest to readers? A special angle that may impress an editor might be based on one particular passion of yours. For instance, if you're a sailor, you might create a how-to-cook-in-a-small-galley-kitchen cookbook.

Remember too that when you are just getting started, it is much easier to build on what you already know, so you will probably want to write the book for readers with a background similar to yours. For example, you know from your own shopping habits which ingredients are too expensive to buy or difficult to find. You even have a feel for the timing of the readers' day and how much time they have to prepare dinner.

On the other hand, your daily experience on the job in a retirement home or with an elderly relative may give you a terrific idea for a seniors' cookbook even though you are young and able. Don't limit yourself if you think you can reach readers who aren't identical to you.

Use Worksheet #1 to evaluate yourself and help determine what kind of cookbook you should write. Apply the questions in the worksheet to the list of the different types of cookbooks above. Where do you see overlap in both your interests and experience? Do you have certain hobbies or are you an expert on a subject that you can apply to one of these categories?

Using the self-knowledge you have gained by working through Worksheet #1, along with the research you will do (see section **b.** below) on what types of books are out there, begin defining and refining your subject.

For instance, what kind of cook are you? Do you enjoy spending a lazy Sunday afternoon preparing a gourmet meal for yourself or your family? Or do you want to spend the least amount of time in the kitchen, yet still prepare healthy, tasty dishes? Your answer to this question will help determine both what your cookbook concept will be, and who your market is.

All the questions on Worksheet #1 prompt you to examine yourself and your experience — experience you can bring to your cookbook. Do you have any specific hobbies or knowledge you can base your cookbook on? Are you a jogger who wants recipes that are high in carbohydrates but low in fat?

What's your culinary training? Have you taken any cooking courses you can apply to your cookbook? Are you proficient at flambéing or pickling? Do you have techniques handed down from your great grandmother you would like to share with readers?

Consider your lifestyle. Are you a traveler who wants to share recipes you've collected on your travels? Or do recipes for cooking over the campfire appeal to you? Also consider your expertise in any area. Are you a dietitian who can apply specialized knowledge to a cookbook? Other factors such as your family, values, ethnic or cultural background, age, and health are also worth considering. Are you allergic to flour? Maybe there's a need for a rice-flour cookbook.

Perhaps one of the most telling question you will answer as you work through Worksheet #1 is, "When you browse the cooking

Worksheet #1
Evaluate yourself

1. What kind of cook are you? _____
_____
_____
_____
_____
_____

2. Hobbies/knowledge base: _____
_____
_____
_____
_____

3. Culinary training: _____
_____
_____
_____
_____

4. Unusual approach to life/unusual experiences/travel: _____
_____
_____
_____
_____

5. Professional perspective/expertise: _____

_____

_____

_____

_____

_____

6. Personal perspective (age, family, values, ethnic/cultural background): _____

_____

_____

_____

_____

_____

7. When you browse the cooking section of a bookstore, what are you hoping to find?

_____

_____

_____

_____

_____

8. Why do you want to write a cookbook? _____

_____

_____

_____

_____

section of a bookstore, what are you hoping to find?" Your answer may indicate a market niche just waiting for you to take advantage of it.

And finally, why do you want to write a cookbook? As you may have realized by now, all these questions and your answers are interrelated. But also take time to consider whether there is any other reason you have not yet defined. Do you want to celebrate your mother's cooking? Pass recipes on to your children? Or perhaps you want to be recognized as a leading expert on cooking with apples. Whatever your answers, they are invaluable in helping you shape your cookbook concept.

b. The competition

One of the first and most important things you need to do once you've decided on a topic or theme is to investigate cookbooks that have already been published. This will allow you to assess your competition as well as get an idea of the different formats and printing and publishing options available to you.

1. Finding cookbooks, in and out of print

Visit your library and local bookstore to check out the competition for your idea. Seeing what's out there may discourage you at first; you may discover ten books very similar in concept to what you thought was your original idea. But take heart. There's almost nothing new when it comes to cooking and eating. Pasta, food fashion's darling for the last decade, born again for generations of Kraft dinner and tuna casserole fans, is actually hundreds of years old. What is new to cookbooks and recipe writing is you — your fresh approach, your original spin on things.

So study all the other cookbooks. Do they handle the subject the way you would, in as much detail as you would like? How would you improve the work? Are the recipes and other text well written? Is the introduction stimulating and exciting? Does the writing make you want to go out, buy some ingredients, and get cooking? Is the book well organized? Is the theme well developed? Are there other books that may be a useful resource for you? Borrow or buy them.

In the bookstores you visit, which publishers' cookbooks are most prominently displayed in the cookbook section? Determining this will give you an idea of the relative strength of some publishers as promoters of their cookbooks, a factor you will want to know later when you determine which, if any, publishers you will approach. (Chapter 8 discusses marketing your cookbook to publishers.)

You should also note which publishers are involved in the type of cookbooks you like. Are they local, American, or Canadian? Are they involved in series publishing and if so, would your cookbook idea work with their publishing program? If you haven't yet decided whether you will approach a publisher or self-publish your cookbook, this is an important first step in making the decision.

Two resources, *Books in Print* and *Canadian Books in Print*, will help you find out about books that may be out of print but still available in the library. Don't overlook these out-of-print books; they often offer valuable ideas.

Use Worksheets #2 and #3 to help you evaluate cookbooks already published. Now that you know what's out there, you can begin to focus more narrowly on what you can offer.

2. What qualities do you like in a cookbook?

Consider your book concept from the reader's point of view. Ask your friends who cook how important each of the following factors are to them when they are using or choosing a cookbook, then use their responses to help you determine what areas you might focus on in your cookbook.

(a) Will they pay more money for high production values (glossy paper, lots of color) or do they prefer not-too-fancy layout with reasonable cost?

(b) Are straightforward dependable recipes more important than recipes that might require more skill or luck but that are spectacular if they succeed?

(c) Is the writing important? Should it be entertaining and informative or is pedestrian writing okay if it's complete and clear?

(d) Is it more important to have a lot of recipes with no illustrations or fewer recipes that are all illustrated in color?

(e) Do they want techniques illustrated as well as described in words?

(f) What recipe format do they prefer? (Ingredients on one side of the page and instructions on the other? Ingredients at the top and instructions below? Ingredients listed in the text? Should recipes run over to a second page? What type size is best?)

Worksheet #2
Researching your book concept: field trip to the library

1. What is my book about? _____

_____

_____

2. Underline three or more KEY WORDS in the description you have written above. You will use these words when you are searching in the indexes of books and magazines, in library catalogues, and on the Internet. Write the words below:

_____

_____

_____

_____

3. What resources do I plan to use to research my book (e.g., books, magazines, journals, radio transcripts, live interviews, the Internet)? _____

_____

_____

_____

What cookbooks have been published in the past that are similar in concept?

Title: _____

Author: _____

Copyright date: _____

Publisher and city of publication: _____

How will my book be different/better? _____

_____

_____

_____

Title: _____

Author: _____

Copyright date: _____

Publisher and city of publication: _____

How will my book be different/better? _____

_____

_____

_____

_____

_____

_____

_____

_____

Title: _____

Author: _____

Copyright date: _____

Publisher and city of publication: _____

How will my book be different/better? _____

_____

_____

_____

_____

_____

_____

_____

_____

Worksheet #3
Researching your book concept: field trip to the bookstore

1. Judging by the new books on display, what are the current trends in cookbook publishing?

_____
_____
_____
_____
_____

2. Which publisher's cookbooks are most prominently displayed in the cookbook section?

_____
_____
_____
_____
_____
_____

3. What cookbooks are currently on the bookstore shelves that are similar in concept to my book (if any)?

Title: _____

Author: _____

Copyright date: _____

Publisher and city of publication: _____

How will my book be different/better? _____

_____
_____
_____

Title: _____

Author: _____

Copyright date: _____

Publisher and city of publication: _____

How will my book be different/better? _____

_____

_____

_____

_____

_____

_____

_____

_____

Title: _____

Author: _____

Copyright date: _____

Publisher and city of publication: _____

How will my book be different/better? _____

_____

_____

_____

_____

_____

_____

_____

(g) Do they like to learn about new techniques and ingredients or do they prerfer to stick with the tried and true?

Analyzing cookbooks will also help get you on the right track. Your favorite cookbook can be a good model for your own book. What qualities does your favorite cookbook have that makes it successful? Worksheet #4 lists the kind of details you need to think through carefully before you begin organizing and writing your cookbook. Apply what you have learned from your close examination of your favorite cookbook (as well as any other cookbooks you choose to evaluate) to your evolving cookbook concept.

c. *Your readership*

1. *Defining your readers*

One of the most important principles in writing is to know your readership. Understanding who is going to read your book will help you every step of the way as you write your cookbook. Knowing your readership is closely intertwined with determining your concept; lamb recipes will not inspire a vegetarian to buy your book. Therefore, you should already have a fairly clear idea of your cookbook's subject and, possibly, its narrower focus (focusing your subject is discussed below in section **d.**). By completing Worksheet #5, you will have a definition of your readership that will keep you on track and prevent you from losing focus once you begin organizing and writing. Keep this definition handy during the cookbook-writing process.

The different ends of the cookbook spectrum, for different readerships:

Frugal cooking for one	or	Elegant dinner parties
Simple organic	or	Recipes of the Russian Royals
Classic farm food	or	New seaweed cookery
Heart-healthy dinners	or	Rich and luscious desserts

Worksheet #4
Analyze your favorite cookbook

Title: _____

Author: _____

Publisher: _____

Copyright date: _____

General concept/theme of this book: _____

_____

_____

Scope of the material: _____

_____

_____

Market/audience for whom it is written: _____

_____

_____

Text (strengths/weaknesses): _____

_____

_____

_____

Design/layout/cover (strengths/weaknesses): _____

_____

_____

Worksheet #4 — Continued

Accessibility of information — how easy is it to find a recipe? _____

_____

_____

Indexes, table of contents (strengths/weaknesses): _____

_____

_____

What makes this book special? What sets it above other books on the same subject? _____

_____

_____

Why is this book useful? _____

_____

_____

_____

How is the subject matter organized? _____

_____

_____

_____

How would I improve the book? _____

_____

_____

_____

Worksheet #5
Defining your audience

Age: _____

Gender: _____

Socioeconomic group(s): _____

_____

_____

_____

_____

Cooking style (check all that apply):

❑ Beginner in the kitchen

❑ Experienced in the kitchen

❑ Gourmet on the weekend

❑ Eats out, cooks for entertainment

❑ Great pride in culinary skills

❑ Cooks out of necessity only

❑ Little knowledge of cooking but curious enough to buy book

❑ Subscribes to culinary magazines

How many meals does reader prepare per day: _____

Per week: _____

Amount of preparation time allowed per meal: _____

_____

_____

_____

Reading level: _____

Book-buying habits: _____

_____

_____

_____

_____

Cookbook-buying habits: _____

_____

_____

_____

_____

_____

Concerns and interests (cooking related and otherwise): _____

_____

_____

_____

_____

_____

_____

_____

_____

_____

_____

2. Research your target group

Once you have defined your readership based on your cookbook concept, you need to research your target group so that you can gear your writing toward that readership. Once you begin to compile and write your cookbook, it is important that you never lose sight of your readers: they should always be foremost in your mind.

How do you find out about your audience? It's simple. Talk to them. Are you writing a book for teenage moms? Seek them out at a local drop-in center. Find out what kind of information they need to make their lives easier. You'll learn a lot.

Do you have a more upscale readership? Talk to these people at the golf course or check out what's on the menu of the chic restaurants they frequent. Read the publications they read such as *Gourmet*, *The New Yorker*, and gardening magazines. What kind of profile can you draw? What do the articles say about the concerns and interests of readers of these magazines? What is the latest food fashion: bean cookery or coffee substitutes? The advertisements can tell you a lot. What are the latest cooking machines? Can you incorporate the readers' information needs into your book?

This is called market research and the more creative you are in determining what information is relevant to your readers, the more useful and successful your book will be. Expand on your answers to Worksheet #5 to assess the age, gender, socioeconomic group, cooking style (experienced or beginner, gourmet or meat-and-potatoes type), reading level, etc., of your audience.

If this is your first book, you will probably find yourself writing for readers of a similar background to yourself. This is much easier. You know from your own shopping habits which ingredients are too fancy or expensive to include in the book. You have a feel for the reader's day and how much time he or she has to throw together dinner.

Chapter 3 discusses compiling your recipes — always with your readers in mind — while chapter 7 discusses writing, and writing to your readers, in more detail.

d. Evaluating and focusing your concept

1. Evaluating your concept

Now that you have evaluated the market and defined your readership, it is time to analyze your own cookbook concept, using Worksheet #6.

Some of the questions you need to ask yourself here are the same as those you asked when you analyzed your favorite cookbook, in Worksheet #4. Worksheet #6 will not only help you focus your subject, but it will also provide you with a useful record of your concept, once again helping to keep you on track.

What is your general concept or theme for the book? Evaluate the scope of the material you plan to have in your cookbook as well as the text. Will you provide extensive history on your cookbook subject? Will there be personal anecdotes? Will the cookbook be text-heavy or will there be mostly recipes and illustrations, with minimal text?

Now is the time to begin focusing your subject, determining which particular areas you want to cover and include and which are beyond the scope of your book. You will have a better idea of this once you have started researching and organizing your book. You should read chapter 3, which discusses the table of contents of your book, before you begin gathering and testing recipes. The table of contents is your skeletal outline and preparing one early on, even if it's only a rough draft subject to change, will let you see how manageable and focused (or big and unwieldy) your book idea is. Having a prepared outline will also help smooth the writing process and prevent any unwanted surprises along the way. If you come across a new topic that might fit your book, you can refer back to the table of contents and see if it is actually relevant. A draft table of contents will also show you obvious gaps in your material that will need to be filled in.

As you analyze your cookbook concept, it is important to again consider the market you are writing for to make sure you have not been sidetracked. Who will your readers be? Will you be writing for people who are on the go, too busy to spend even an hour preparing a dish, or will your book be aimed at the gourmet who relishes spending an afternoon in the kitchen? You will already know the market for your cookbook from the research you did in section c. and for Worksheet #5.

Although the book design, layout, and cover are often a trade publisher's decision, your input is valuable. Having an idea of these things at the outset of your project will also help keep you focused in your writing. For instance, do you envision pages with lots of white space, perhaps with sidebars or tips running in the margins? If you do, now is the time to start collecting those tips and tidbits.

Worksheet #6
Analyze your cookbook concept

General concept/theme of this book: _____

_____

_____

_____

_____

_____

Market/audience for whom it is written: _____

_____

_____

_____

_____

Scope of the material: _____

_____

_____

_____

_____

_____

Text: _____

_____

_____

_____

_____

_____

Design/layout/cover: _____

_____

_____

_____

_____

What makes this book special? What sets it above other books on the same subject? _____

_____

_____

_____

_____

Will I have an index and table of contents? _____

_____

_____

_____

How will the subject matter be organized? _____

_____

_____

_____

_____

_____

_____

_____

If you plan to self-publish your cookbook, you will likely be in control of the design, layout, and cover of the book. Write down your ideas now. Remember, you can always rework them later.

What makes your book special? You will have an idea of what sets it above other books on the same subject from your research trips to the library and bookstores. Recording this information will help you keep focused as you organize and then write the material.

How is the subject matter organized? Will you have an index and table of contents? These are factors to keep in mind as you continue the cookbook-writing process. Chapters 3 and 7 discuss the organization, including the table of contents and index, further.

2. Protect your ideas

Ideas are a writer's savings account. Protect yours until you're ready to promote them. Then tell the world.

Don't forget that there is a downside to good ideas — they don't stay yours for long. Anyone in business will tell you that once someone comes up with a good idea, others will be quick to copy it. Although it is not possible to copyright an idea alone, but only the expression of that idea, it is still a good idea to be prudent while developing your cookbook concept.

Ideas are a writer's savings account. Protect yours and don't spread them around until you're at the stage where you want to promote them. Then tell the world.

3. Know when to abandon an idea

After studying your market, whether it's local, regional (state or provincial), national, or international, you may find that it is saturated with one or many similar books.

Do your homework. It is possible to sell a book in a regional context even if it has no national appeal. It's also possible to take a proven local idea and sell it to a wider readership.

But also be realistic. It may seem hard to throw out an idea in which you have invested time, but it is better to bail out now before far greater amounts of time and money have been spent. You're not giving up the idea of writing a cookbook or giving up the idea of being a writer. You're just letting go of one idea. There are lots more where that one came from.

2
Cookbooks as community fund-raisers: a group effort

S can your shelves. You probably have at least five community
cookbooks. You probably bought them from friends in the same
spirit that you annually buy Girl Guide cookies or school chocolates — to support the organizations' causes. You may have even
bought one book on a trip to some rural corner of North America.
Perhaps you thought you'd catch a bit of the local flavor, be it
regional Maritime lobster chowder or an insider's secret method of
making perogies.

With a collective product you have a marketing edge, a captive
audience. Many people will initially buy your book because they
want to support your cause. They will be delighted if they discover
that the cookbook is much more than a charity cookbook with a few
well-worn recipes.

Another big selling point for a community cookbook is that many
people will feel a part of the book and want to share it with others.

Aunt Bessie will be thrilled to see her name in print: Aunt Bessie's Plum Pudding. All of Aunt Bessie's nieces, nephews, children, and grandchildren will want a copy.

When writing a community cookbook, you have a responsibility to produce something that reflects the group. Include lots of personal anecdotes and local touches. You might also want to include:

- Family photographs
- Photographs of local architecture
- Historical anecdotes
- Humor
- Stories
- Poetry
- Kitchen secrets

Your cookbook can be anything you want it to be, and with a little effort, it will be a real gem. It includes the contributions of not just a few people but a community with a history, intelligence, and heart of its own.

To be successful, your effort must have all the qualities of a professionally produced book. These include an attractive cover and a good concept with logically organized, easily accessible information. The recipes must be tested to guarantee results. Above all, the writers must care about their work.

But the book does not need to be glossy and sophisticated. What you want to sell is what you do best. What does your group stand for? Are your functions renowned for good food?

All the chapters in this book — from generating an idea for the cookbook, to researching and collecting recipes, to writing about food, to printing and promoting the book — will be useful to you and the committee. Some aspects of writing a community cookbook, however, are only relevant to community cookbook committees. This chapter will start you on your way to organizing your committees and approaching the community for recipes.

a. More ideas for community cookbooks

Chapter 1 started you thinking about the different types of cookbooks and the various subjects and focuses of cookbooks. Typically, community cookbooks focus on the following topics.

A community cookbook includes the contributions of not just a few people but a community with a history, intelligence, and heart of its own.

- Ethnic recipes (e.g., old country ways, adaptations to new ingredients)
- Recipes of the region (e.g., southern cooking)
- Dinners teenagers can make for the family
- Favorites for any age (e.g., preschoolers, elementary school, elderly patients at senior homes)
- Our favorite family Christmas, barbecues, etc.
- Themes that reflect your community (e.g., grain farmers' bread book, best sandwich recipes from church teas)

b. Cookbook by committee

Before you begin the project, get a group of enthusiastic and cooperative people together and divide the work into committees. One person can do more than one job, depending on the size of your cookbook and the time available.

Although the work of some of these committees — the publicity committee and the inventory and sales committee, for example — will not be done until later on, once the cookbook is closer to being published or has actually been published, there are some tasks these committees can start on now. For instance, planning book launches and tours can, and should, begin before the book is actually printed.

1. Publishing committee

To form your publishing committee, you'll first need a chair or possibly two people to cochair. The chair's responsibility is to coordinate the whole project as well as oversee the activities of the editorial committee.

The chair may take the role of writer or assign this role to another member of the committee. The writer will write the nonrecipe text of the manuscript. Depending on your concept, you may need large chunks of text written and edited, as for any book. Consider that at the very minimum you will need an introduction to the book, chapter introductions, and introductions to each recipe.

The publishing committee has certain responsibilities:
- Developing a concept
- Providing continuity from beginning to end
- Making financial decisions, including a budget
- Communicating with members of other committees

Six key committees:

- Publishing committee
- Recipe editing and testing committee
- Production committee
- Proofreading committee
- Publicity committee
- Inventory and sales committee

- Researching printing options and making decisions on a printer for the book
- Setting deadlines
- Soliciting donations of services and supplies
- Setting up an office
- Choosing computer word processing and publishing software
- Writing and editing nonrecipe text of book

As well, certain decisions need to be made at the beginning of the project. The publishing committee must decide on —

(a) a process for recipe selection: i.e., will the committee be able to refuse a recipe?

(b) a style and format of recipe to be used (this can involve establishing contributor guidelines. See chapter 4 for a detailed discussion of recipe style.);

(c) the number of recipes to be used; and

(d) a schedule for the project.

If your cookbook is a community cookbook, you will likely depend on members of your community or your particular organization to contribute the recipes. The next chapter will also be helpful to you, as it discusses other sources of recipes that may be appropriate to your project and that you therefore may want to consider.

Samples #1 and #2 show two form letters that can be used to solicit recipes from the community. You can model yours on these or just use the ideas that are suitable for your particular project. Sample #3 is a sample follow-up letter mailed out once the committee has made contact with members of the community or organization that will be contributing recipes. Sample #4 shows a recipe form you would include with the follow-up letter. Such a form will help standardize contributors' submissions and also ensures that contributors don't leave out important instructions.

2. Recipe editing and testing committee

You will also need to form a recipe editing and testing committee. This may be two committees if you wish. It's usually best to have a fairly large committee for recipe testing, to share the workload.

The recipe editing and testing committee responsibilities are —

(a) reading, rewriting, and editing recipes;

(b) verifying information with recipe contributor, where necessary; and

Sample #1
Letter #1 to members soliciting help with cookbook project

Cookbook Committee
Baycrest Church
101 Cook Street
Baycrest, WA 98225
May 10, 199-

Dear members,

At the turn of the last century, the ground was turned for a small woodframe structure which was to become our spiritual home for 100 years.

Here we are at the turn of the millennium and over five generations have been baptized in our church. Five generations have attended services every Sunday.

Unfortunately, wooden structures do not fare as well as spiritual institutions. Our building has grown and has been lovingly renovated. But once again we find ourselves needing to raise $20,000 for new clapboard.

We have come up with a very special fund-raising project. What is the glue that binds cultural and family traditions, that sustains us body and soul? Food, of course. We know that there is a wealth of recipes out there and we want to bring them together into one cookbook that we can sell to raise money for the church.

We would like you to dig down deep into your recipes boxes and those of older relatives to find the oldest recipes you can, perhaps some as old as our church.

Please write a paragraph telling us something about the recipe. Where did it come from? Do you have childhood memories about this dish?

Enclosed are forms to be filled in with your recipes. We're hoping to receive three recipes from each member. We're also expecting that you'll be able to sell at least ten copies of the book once it's published.

Our committee is meeting soon and we're looking for help. Can you type? Test recipes? Solicit advertising? Please call Marie at 555-0909.

Someone from the committee will be calling you within a week to see what recipes you will be able to contribute.

Thanks so much for your support.

Yours sincerely,

Cookbook committee

Sample #2
Letter #2 to members soliciting help with cookbook project

Cookbook Committee
12 Savory Lane
Baycrest, WA 98225
May 10, 199-

Dear parents,

We're going camping! That's what scouts do, right? Then why this letter? We're going camping . . . halfway round the world, to the big jamboree in Australia. That means fund-raising, and we want to tell you about our project that the boys and girls have thought up themselves.

We are writing a camping cookbook. Included will be recipes for cooking over fires, on barbecues, in pits; recipes for things like clams steamed in seaweed over a bonfire, chicken on a spit, and beef stew in a cast-iron pot. It's true that almost anything tastes good when it's eaten outside, but there are certain tricks, methods, and ingredients that we hope you will share with us.

Each scout will bring in three recipes which parents will help test at home. They will hand write and illustrate each recipe. These will all be laser scanned by Jill and Joe Mackie, Daniel's parents, who own a desktop publishing center.

The cookbook will be a terrific memento for the group and, we hope, an excellent cookbook. As we're planning to sell 1,000 copies, we need each parent to sell 35. It's a winning combination: kids motivated with a goal, an excellent project, and committed parents.

You'll be hearing more details in our next letter. We'll keep you posted. In the meantime, why not try cooking dinner in the fireplace tonight?

Yours sincerely,

Cookbook committee

Sample #3
Follow-up letter to members contributing recipes

Recipe Committee
Grand Forks Keep Fit Society
1110 Apple Drive
Baycrest, WA 98225
April 8, 199-

Dear members,

The cookbook committee of Grand Forks Keep Fit Society is pleased that you will be able to contribute recipes from your personal collection.

Enclosed are forms that we would like you to fill out. Using this format will make it easier for our keyboarding volunteers. If you wish to hand in a computer printout of your recipe, please follow this format. Also attached for your reference is a sample recipe that illustrates our recipe style guidelines.

We are looking for recipes that are specially adapted by you, not copied word-for-word from a book. We prefer that you use the freshest, healthiest ingredients rather than processed foods.

We ask that you test the recipe at least once and measure carefully. We want to ensure that our readers will be able to duplicate your results.

Our book title is *The Keep Fit Society's Book of Healthy Eating* and so we are looking for recipes on a theme of healthy, low-fat meals.

Our deadline is approaching so we would like to receive your recipes by May 8, 199-.

Please call Marie at 555-0690 if you have any questions.

We appreciate your contribution.

Thank you,

Recipe committee

RECIPE FORM

Recipe from the kitchen of: _____

Passed down from: _____

A creative adaptation based on a recipe from _____ *cookbook*

Title of recipe: _____

Introduction: (Use 25 words or less. Perhaps a personal recommendation, a family anecdote, or serving instructions. Use your imagination to entice readers to try your recipe.)

_____

_____

_____

_____

_____

_____

List of ingredients in order used: (Please measure! Both imperial and metric please.)

_____

_____

_____

_____

_____

_____

_____

_____

_____

_____

Method: (Clear, numbered steps. Please start phrase with verb such as combine, place, cream. Specify size of bowl, pan, skillet as small, medium, large.)

_____

_____

_____

_____

_____

_____

_____

_____

_____

_____

_____

Results: (Specify number of servings where possible.) _____

_____

_____

Your name: _____

Address: _____

_____

Telephone number where we can reach you to verify facts: _____

Please return this form to Marie Chow by May 8, 199-.

Please call Marie at 555-0690 if you have any questions.

(c) testing recipes, if that is part of process.

(a) To test or not to test

If you are writing a cookbook by yourself, you naturally maintain a level of integrity by testing and retesting each and every recipe — your name on the book implies a personal guarantee that the recipes work. Working in a group is different. The recipes may be contributed by many different sources: great cooks, lousy cooks, vegans, and junk food lovers. It's a potluck of recipes. Decisive editing is essential.

Ask contributors to test their recipes, to measure accurately, and to clearly describe their results. Provide recipe style guidelines; ask contributors to submit recipes on specific forms the production committee has designed.

Testing recipes by committee will guarantee some degree of uniformity throughout the collection. But it can be an expensive activity, prohibitively so. Budget to pay for testing ingredients along with all the other publication expenses. Estimate a ballpark figure, for example, $10 per recipe. Perhaps you can solicit donations from local grocery stores or ask members to donate ingredients.

Another good way to test recipes is to have a potluck dinner where members bring their recipes and prepared dishes. Have members fill in comment sheets (see chapter 6 for more on taste testing).

3. Production committee

While community cookbooks are usually self-published, occasionally a trade publisher is interested in publishing such a book or is interested in buying the rights to a best-selling cookbook and then redesigning and distributing the book. Unless you have interest from a trade publisher, you will likely design and produce the cookbook yourself.

The responsibilities of the production committee are —
(a) creating recipe forms,
(b) receiving completed recipe forms and keying them into the computer, and
(c) formatting the recipes using publishing software.

4. Proofreading committee

The proofreading committee is responsible for receiving the printouts of the laid-out manuscript from the production committee and

Ask contributors to test their recipes, to measure accurately, and to clearly describe their results.

Consider soliciting donations from local grocery stores or ask members to donate ingredients to help reduce expense.

checking them to eliminate typographical errors. Chapter 7 discusses editing and proofreading in more detail.

5. Publicity committee

The publicity committee's responsibilities for promoting the book include:

    (a) planning a book launch,

    (b) organizing special events,

    (c) handling advertising,

    (d) arranging media interviews for editor and other involved members,

    (e) sending out review copies and press kits,

    (f) doing direct mail order mailouts, and

    (g) planning a book tour.

See chapter 9 for more on how to promote your cookbook.

6. Inventory and sales committee

The inventory and sales committee is responsible for —

    (a) contacting members about orders,

    (b) contacting nonmembers (e.g., bookstores) about orders,

    (c) creating sales forms, and taking and filing orders,

    (d) picking up and storing inventory,

    (e) packaging orders to be mailed, and

    (f) delivering books to bookstores, members, and other points of sale.

You might also want to have a separate advertising sales committee to sell sponsorships or advertising to offset the cost of production. Or this task could be incorporated into the duties of the inventory and sales committee.

Now read on to discover how to choose a recipe style, write a table of contents, and put sparkle into your food writing!

3
Collecting recipes

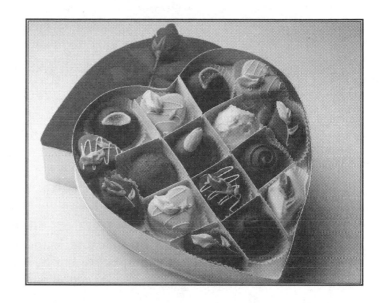

Once you have decided on the concept of your cookbook, you need to begin the process of gathering the recipes you will include in your book. As discussed in chapter 1, there are many different cookbook concepts, and the concept you decide on will, in part, help determine your source of recipes. For example, if you plan to write a cookbook of recipes gathered from the community or celebrities, or if you own a restaurant or deli and want your cookbook to consist of recipes of your offerings, your source of recipes will be obvious.

a. Creating an outline: your table of contents

The table of contents is the first thing to write, and the last. You'll need to write one if you plan to approach a publisher with a book proposal (more about this in chapter 8). You also need to write one as a bare skeleton of your book, a plan of where you're going, even if you intend to self-publish. The outline you create now will eventually become the table of contents for your book.

Use the outline to organize the recipes. The sooner you have an idea of the way in which you want to organize your recipes, the better. Your outline will guide you through the collecting, researching, writing, and editing stages.

Consider your first table of contents as a draft. As you write your book, adding, deleting, altering, and incorporating editor's suggestions, your contents page will evolve as well. Change is inevitable as you develop more and more recipes and continue learning through your research. Refine as you go. You don't have to stick rigidly to your outline; stray where necessary or desirable — just make sure it *is* necessary or desirable.

The contents page reflects the logic of the book. There are various standard styles for tables of contents. The most traditional pattern for organizing recipes (i.e., starting with appetizers and salads and working through the stages of a meal to desserts) makes sense for general encyclopedic collections but may not for yours. Choose the order that makes the most sense for your type of cookbook.

As you continue through the process of researching, writing, and editing, natural subdivisions within your outline will become clearer. For example, you may decide to subdivide your section on entrées into chapters on fish, poultry, and meat, or your section on pasta into chapters on fettucine, gnocchi, lasagna, and linguine.

Sometimes you may not be able to decide on an order for your table of contents or you may not be able to create a detailed one until you have gathered most of your recipes and done the bulk of your research. If your cookbook features a single ingredient or type of food, for example, apples or candy, you may not be able to see the natural subdivisions until you have all, or most of, the recipes.

Having said this, it is still important to know at this early stage of writing your cookbook the different ways in which you can organize your book.

1. Encyclopedic

Below is the table of contents for a cookbook organized in a standard encyclopedic style.

Chapter 1	Appetizers
Chapter 2	Soups
Chapter 3	Main dishes
Chapter 4	Salads

Table of contents styles:

- Encyclopedic
- Alphabetic
- Meal planner
- Cooking method
- Seasonal
- By ingredient
- Geographical distribution

Your cookbook is your unique concept and it may not fit well into this template of subject chapters. A book on vegetarian cooking for children might very well suit this format. But how would you subdivide a book on candy?

The objective of a table of contents is to guide readers to the information they are seeking. Try to make your table as logical, clear, and easy to understand as possible. Start with the body of knowledge you have gathered and look for natural subdivisions of subject. For example, start by looking up a definition of candy in the dictionary. You may find something like:

> **Candy** 1: *crystallized sugar formed by boiling down sugar syrup.* 2: *a confection made with sugar and often flavoring and filling.*

A thesaurus lists many names of candy: bonbon, brittle, bubble gum, butterscotch, candied apple, candy corn, caramel, chewing gum, chocolate, chocolate bar, chocolate drop, cotton candy, cough drop, cream, divinity, fondant fudge, glacé, gum, gumdrop, hard candy, honey crisp, horehound, jelly bean, jelly egg, jujube, kiss, licorice, Life Saver, lollipop, lozenge, marshmallow, marzipan, mint, nougat, peanut bar, peanut brittle, penuche, peppermint, popcorn balls, praline, rock candy, saltwater taffy, Scotch kisses, sugar candy, sugarplum, taffy, toffee, torrone, and tutti-frutti.

If you had to group them according to kind, how would you do it? Here are some suggestions:

- Medicinal candies with herbs such as mint, and cough drops

- Texture: creamy, hard, soft, chewy, jellied

- Variations on a single type: chocolates with nuts, cream centers, fruit fillings

- Degree of complexity: from simple popcorn balls to the just-about-impossible-to-make-at-home bubble gum
- Ingredients: coconut, chocolate, nuts
- Geography: candy of Sri Lanka, Norway
- History: candy from each decade of the 20th century

There's no right or wrong way. But there is a logical and illogical way. You must decide what is logical and what will make the recipes most accessible to your readers.

2. Alphabetic

A second way to organize your table of contents is in alphabetical order. This is another standard table of contents format. Using the candy cookbook example from the previous section, you might organize the table of contents as shown below if you were to use the alphabetic style.

- Butterscotch
- Candied apple
- Candy corn
- Caramel
- Chocolate
- Fudge
- Hard candy
- Lollipop
- Marshmallow
- Marzipan
- Mints
- Nougat
- Peanut brittle
- Penuche
- Popcorn balls
- Praline
- Rock candy
- Saltwater taffy

3. Meal planner: breakfast, lunch, supper

The meal planner table of contents is a more comprehensive approach to organizing recipes or groups of recipes than either the encyclopedic or alphabetic style. The meal planner style often includes whole menus.

This kind of cookbook tries to answer questions such as, "What should I make for dinner?" or, "What should I take to the picnic?" This style of organization is used in cookbooks for entertaining where the author speaks from personal experiences.

The meal planner style of organization is similar to the standard encyclopedic style. The headings below were those I used in a book I wrote on apples. They illustrate how a single-ingredient cookbook about apples was organized using the meal planner style.

- Apple varieties
- Cooking with apples
- Apples for breakfast, brunch, and lunch
- Apples at tea
- Apples for dinner
- Apples for dessert

This table of contents style is useful when you are determining how many recipes you need and trying to balance each section within the cookbook.

4. Cooking method

Dividing up the subject matter by cooking method is useful in certain circumstances such as meat cookery, where the cook would probably start by bringing home a cut of meat from the store and then try to figure out what to with it. For example:

Chapter 1	Roasting
Chapter 2	Grilling, broiling
Chapter 3	Poaching
Chapter 4	Braising, soups, and stews
Chapter 5	Oven baking, casseroles, and loaves
Chapter 6	Frying
Chapter 7	Curing and pickling
Chapter 8	Barbecuing

5. Seasonal

A cookbook organized by season would have sections corresponding to spring, summer, fall, and winter. For example —

Chapter 1	Winter soups and stews
Chapter 2	Spring tonics: greens and berries
Chapter 3	Summer garden reverie: herbs and pies
Chapter 4	Fall cornucopia
Chapter 5	Celebration dinners

6. By ingredient

A herb cookbook lends itself well to being organized by type of ingredient. Your table of contents may look something like this:

Chapter 1	Sage
Chapter 2	Savory
Chapter 3	Thyme
Chapter 4	Rosemary
Chapter 5	Mint
Chapter 6	Caraway

7. Geographical distribution

Regional and ethnic cookbooks are naturals for organization based on where dishes originated rather than on what they are made of. A table of contents based on geographical distribution may look something like this —

Chapter 1	Newfoundland recipes
Chapter 2	Maritime cooks
Chapter 3	French Canadian cookery
Chapter 4	Upper Canada fare
Chapter 5	Prairie feasts
Chapter 6	Wild Pacific Northwest
Chapter 7	Northern touches

Worksheet #7 will help you determine the best style in which to organize your book.

b. *How many recipes do you need?*

The number of recipes you need to test and include in your book depends on the scope of your book. If you already have a publisher, it will probably set guidelines immediately about the number of pages you need to fill and the number of recipes required. Publishers research publishing trends and understand the vagaries of consumer taste in cookbooks. They know, for example, that quality paperbacks are popular, that big print is good for an aging population, and that the targeted consumer won't pay more than a certain price for a cookbook.

If you are self-publishing, you have more control over how many recipes will be included in the book. Consider both your budget and your time. Look at published cookbooks similar to how you envision yours and see how many recipes they contain.

The outline or preliminary table of contents that you have drafted will also help you determine how many recipes you need. By creating a logical structure to your book, you will be able to more clearly see the divisions and balance of recipes. For example, if you are organizing your cookbook in a menu planner style, you will likely want to have approximately the same number of recipes for each section: appetizer, soup and salad, entrées, dessert. Going one step farther, you may want to divide entrées into subsections of pasta, meat, and fish, and collect an equal number of recipes for each subsection. Remember that your outline can always change — you are not locked into any decision you make at this stage, but you should always try to achieve some sort of balance amongst your recipes.

It is always a good idea, where economically possible, to have more recipes than you need for the final cut. This allows you to discard recipes that don't work without having to scramble to find replacement recipes.

c. *Sourcing recipes*

It used to be that good cooks jealously guarded their recipes. The secret ingredient that changed Mrs. Norton's Potato Scallop from an

1. What is my cookbook about? Summarize the subject of the cookbook. _____

_____

_____

_____

2. What kinds of recipes will I include? How many of each? _____

_____

_____

_____

_____

3. What reader's questions do I hope to answer? Describe the natural and logical flow of ideas in the book. _____

_____

_____

4. What are the natural subdivisions of my subject?_____

_____

_____

_____

5. What's the best format for my subject matter?

❏ Standard encyclopedic

❏ Alphabetic

❏ Meal planner: breakfast, lunch, supper

❏ Cooking method

❏ Seasonal: spring, summer, fall, winter

❏ By ingredient

❏ Geographical distribution

❏ Other

everyday bland mass to the envy of the church potluck supper was (you'll never guess) tarragon!

Today, people seem far less possessive of their recipes, probably because printed recipes are everywhere now, handed out at the store with the promotion of a new product, in the fall lineup of new Christmas books, in magazines at every grocery checkout. The kitchen is no longer the sole domain of Mom who takes great pride in her contribution to the bake sale. People are more relaxed about cooking; cooking has become an entertainment, a pastime. Recipes are passed quite naturally from one person to another. The motive is simple: the sharing of food is a pleasure basic to humanity.

Even so, you do need to be aware of copyright law. People do own recipes that are published under copyright law.

Recipes are passed quite naturally from one person to another. The motive is simple: the sharing of food is a pleasure basic to humanity.

1. Copyright

If recipes are essentially your own, there is no problem with copyright: you own them. If you adopt another person's idea for a recipe but not that person's expression of it, you are in a gray area. Although ideas alone cannot be copyrighted, you should ask yourself, "Is my recipe recognizable as another person's idea?"

Of course I'm assuming it is not your intention to lift someone else's work, word-for-word, phrase-for-phrase, and to sell it as your own. That would be immoral as well as illegal. You do not want to plagiarize, just as you wouldn't want someone else to plagiarize your work. If you want to use another writer's recipe, write that author asking his or her permission (or the publisher's permission) to do so.

If you are publishing your cookbook with a trade publisher (discussed in more detail in chapter 8), your publisher may have a form letter you can use. Sample #5 shows a sample request for permission to reprint material.

You may be granted permission under certain conditions. For example, you may be required to compensate the author financially or to give that author credit in the introduction or elsewhere in your book. When in doubt about whether you need to seek permission to use a recipe, consult a lawyer versed in copyright.

2. Recipes from experts

In the course of your research (discussed in detail in chapter 7), you may interview experts in the industry or experts on a specific subject that is the focus of your cookbook. Don't overlook these

Jane Smith
123 Birch Street
Townsville, BC V0E 0E0
September 12, 199-

Lynn Baker
556 Scott Row
Winnipeg, MB K1L 4H9

RE: PERMISSION TO REPRINT MATERIAL

Dear Ms. Baker:

I am writing a book tentatively titled *Homemade Pies* which will be published by Pie Press in the fall of 199-. The book will retail for $17.95.

I am requesting your permission to include the excerpt (recipe) described below in any and all editions of my book. Please indicate the acknowledgment you would like printed in the book.

Enclosed is a duplicate copy of this letter for your files and a stamped self-addressed envelope for your convenience. Thank you for your prompt response.

Yours sincerely,

Jane Smith

Sample #5 — Continued

MATERIAL TO BE REPRINTED

Title of book: Best of the Sea

Author: Lynn Baker

Publisher: Random Press

ISBN: 6-67676-676-6

Copyright: 199-

Owner of Copyright: Lynn Baker

Description: page 3   Line 1 to page 3 Line 30

Recipe title: Bumbleberry Pie

Permission granted by: _____

_____

Acknowledgments to read: _____

_____

_____

_____

_____

_____

---

experts as a source of recipes. They are often eager to share. But be sure you get their explicit permission to reprint their recipe.

3. Recipes from nonexperts

As with recipes from experts, be sure you obtain permission to reproduce any recipe you collect from your nonexpert sources. When collecting recipes from nonexperts, you may wish to reproduce all or some of the instructions verbatim to retain the flavor of the language (e.g., Grandma's "rub in butter the size of a small walnut").

You should, however, test the recipe and rewrite if necessary to guarantee predictable results. Watch out that you don't lose anything in efficient recipe writing. You may eliminate steps because they seem unnecessary. For example, Aunt Flo may have punched down her bread three times during rising, but you think a modern cook would lose patience with this. Be careful: the texture of your bread probably won't be quite as chewy as Aunt Flo's. Chapter 6 discusses testing recipes in more detail.

4. Your own recipes

Undoubtedly you will have some of your own recipes — those handed down from your mother or grandmother or even great grandmother, as well as those you have created yourself — that you plan to include in your book. But don't overlook the fact that there's a wealth of cooking knowledge out there — and not just in cookbooks. You'll find culinary advice, recipes, and food traditions in history books, gardening books, even encyclopedias. Chapter 7 discusses the four steps of writing: researching, interviewing, writing, and editing. It also offers further tips on where and how to source recipes. But first, chapter 4 will take you step by step through the components of a recipe — basic knowledge you will need to be able to develop your food writing.

When collecting recipes from nonexperts, you may wish to reproduce all or some of the instructions verbatim to retain the flavor of the language.

4
The recipes

a. A recipe is . . .

A recipe is a set of instructions for making something from specific ingredients. It has the same Latin root (*recipere*) as the word "receive." In the past, the terms "receipt" and "recipe" were used interchangeably. The first recipes were inventory lists in military camps where a written list was required to order foodstuffs. Recipes are like folktales. They tell a story that is passed down from one generation to the next.

> *By setting aside a day for feasting and sharing ritual foods with our neighbors, we renew our bonds to our community. When we prepare dishes handed down to us from our grandmothers, we become grandchildren again, reconnected to the people who have gone before us. When we prepare traditional food for our children, we give them memories they can turn to when they are grown and cut adrift. They will prepare these foods and once again be grounded with their families in time.*
>
> excerpted from Judith Comfort's Christmas Cookbook, Doubleday, 1988.

A cookbook can be many wonderful things. It can be a history book or a biography. But first and foremost, it is a technical manual. Recipe writing is a type of technical writing that loosely follows the scientific method, perfected when home economics was evolving as a science, complete with labs and Bunsen burners.

Scientific method:	Recipe method:
Purpose	Introduction
Hypothesis	List of ingredients
Materials	Instructions/method
Procedure	Yield
Results and observations	Testing
Conclusion	
Discussion and error analysis	

b. Good recipe writing

You may want to wax poetic in your introduction of the "best chocolate cake I ever ate," conjure up appetizing images, inspire readers to run to the kitchen to start sifting flour and cocoa. But when you write a recipe, you should be dead serious if you care about readers being able to duplicate your results. It doesn't matter how homey or upscale the design of a book, or how fashionable the ingredients. The phrase that needs to spring from your readers' lips to give you the word-of-mouth publicity that guarantees a second printing of your book is, "The recipes are really good, clearly written, easy to follow."

This may sound boring. But if you analyze the dozen or more cookbooks on your kitchen shelf, the ones with the well-worn pages are the ones that have recipes that work every single time. They have become part of your life.

Communication from one cook to another is accomplished with good technical writing.

Communication from one cook to another is accomplished with good technical writing. Technical writing is found everywhere, from surgeons' manuals on how to do open-heart surgery to the booklet that came with your computer. Good technical writing eschews incomprehensible jargon and is well illustrated, cross-referenced, and has a detailed table of contents, glossary, and index. These are the qualities you should aspire to in your recipe writing and in compiling your cookbook.

1. Accurate and precise

Testing your recipes guarantees accuracy. The integrity of your book depends on testing. Using standards of measurement adds precision. "A pinch of this or that" is a relative term and not reliable. For consistent results, use standard measurements such as "⅛ teaspoon (.5 mL)." Appendix 1 lists and defines standard cooking terms. Appendix 4 lists standard terminology for instructions. Use them as you write your recipes.

2. Clear

Hold the evocative and obscure terms. Comprehension is all. Use small, descriptive words instead of big words. Use short, to-the-point phrases instead of long-winded explanations. If you do choose to write in a more anecdotal than scientific style, try to be as graphic and unambiguous as possible. Leave nothing to the imagination.

Clearly lay out the cooking process in logical steps or paragraphs. If you need to say something that doesn't quite fit into the recipe but is still useful, place it in the introduction, or in a sidebar.

3. Targeted

Don't ever forget the audience that you are writing for — a cookbook is a type of user's manual. Make sure that your recipes are user-friendly!

4. Concise

There are dozens of ways to write a recipe, from long-winded personal paragraphs to cryptically short, point-form sentences that are bound to fail. Strike a balance. Be as brief as you can, but be sure to give enough information for concise clarity.

5. Complete

In the rush to be concise, don't leave anything out. I find that it is best to start with too much information and then pare it down. It's usually easier and safer to edit something than to find and insert a missing step.

6. Consistent

This sounds obvious, but you shouldn't call something a pot at the beginning of a recipe and a pan at the end. It will only confuse your readers. Make choices between metric and imperial (or decide if you will use both) and all the other style choices (discussed in section **d.**

There are a number of qualities of good recipe writing. Good recipe writing is —

- Accurate and precise
- Clear
- Targeted
- Concise
- Complete
- Consistent

below), and stick to them. When choosing between systems of measurements, keep in mind that Canadians often use both metric and imperial, Europeans use metric, and Americans use imperial measurement that varies slightly from the British imperial system. While it may be some publishers' house style to give measurements in both imperial and metric, it is important that you make your decision and use it consistently.

Again, you may want to refer to Appendixes 1 and 4 for the standard terms used in recipes and food writing. Appendix 2 lists the standard measurements and metric-imperial conversions, while Appendix 3 gives liquid and dry volume equivalents.

c. Parts of a recipe

While there are many styles in writing recipes (see section **d.** below), a common terminology is used to describe the parts of a recipe. Figure #1 shows an outline of the parts of a recipe.

1. Title

Choose a title that is interesting and inspiring to readers, and one that accurately describes the dish. Avoid using cute or coy titles. No one will know what Hawaiian Surprise is, but they *will* be able to picture a Pineapple Soufflé.

2. Introduction

The introduction is the place to entice a reader to try the recipe. Use your creative skills here. Information you might want to put in an introduction includes:

- A personal recommendation ("The best chocolate cake I ever tasted")
- Suggestions for serving ("Goes well with . . .")
- Hints about settings or occasions to which the recipe is well suited ("Ideal for that ski weekend in the mountains")
- Comments on preparation ("This soup tastes best if you make it the night before")
- Advice about storage ("Freezes well")
- Suggestions for serving ("Great served with a crusty French baguette")

Parts of a recipe:

- Title
- Introduction
- List of ingredients
- Instructions/ method
- Yield

Figure #1
Parts of a recipe

Title:

Corned beef on rye pudding

Introduction:

entice the reader

If you are a fan of corned beef on rye and enjoy bread pudding, try this delicious combination. It's out of this world!

List of ingredients:

order of use

6 slices stale rye bread

1 cup (250 mL) corned beef, chopped

1 cup (250 mL) cheddar cheese, cubed

3 eggs

1 tsp. (5 mL) Dijon mustard

1 Tbsp. (15 mL) onion, grated

¼ tsp. (1 mL) nutmeg

3 cups (750 mL) hot milk

Instructions/method:

chronological and logical order

Cut bread into quarters. Place half the bread in greased 8-inch (2 L) square cake pan. Top with corned beef and cheese.

In bowl, beat eggs, mustard, onion, and nutmeg. Gradually whisk in hot milk. Pour half the mixture over bread in dish. Top with remaining bread and drizzle on remaining mixture.

visual imagery

Bake in 325°F (165°C) oven for about 50 minutes or until <u>slightly puffed and browned</u>. Serve hot.

Yield:

6 servings

3. List of ingredients

List ingredients in the order they will be used. Describe them as they are normally purchased. For example, you would describe chocolate by the number of squares, beans by weight or can size (remember to specify whether canned beans are drained or not), cheese by the pound (unless it is grated, in which case it's measured by volume), and garlic by number of cloves.

For unusual or exotic ingredients, it's a good idea to suggest places they might be sold ("Wasabi can be found in most Japanese food stores").

For unusual or exotic ingredients, it's a good idea to suggest places they might be sold.

Most writers list ingredients only once, even if they are to be divided and used at different times in the recipe, although you might choose to list each ingredient as it is used. Your choice is between a cleaner, shorter ingredient list (e.g., "1½ cups [375 mL] flour") and a longer one, possibly taking two lines ("1 cup [250 mL] flour" and "½ cup [125 mL] flour"). Listing the ingredient twice takes more room, but it also makes it less likely for the reader to mistakenly add the total amount of flour called for instead of the required portion. On the other hand, it can cause confusion when the reader is making a grocery list and has to add up the ingredients twice.

The point to remember is that it doesn't matter what style you use as long as you are consistent from one recipe to another. Readers will adjust to whichever style you choose.

4. Instructions/method

Describe the food preparation in steps, chronologically and logically. If there are steps that can be performed ahead of time, list them near the beginning; cooks appreciate knowing this information before they begin the recipe. Very few books mention preparation time since this is quite subjective.

Most recipes include the following steps in the method:
- (a) Beginning: oven temperature and cooking time/preheating oven, assembling utensils for cooking (pots, pans)
- (b) Middle: combining, cooking
- (c) End: garnishing, serving

Try to keep the preparing and cooking of food in the instructions/method part of the recipe. However, it is often a good idea to include prepared or cooked food in the list of ingredients (e.g., "1 cup [250 mL] chopped carrots"). This makes the recipe more accurate and also simplifies the method (rather than instructing in the body of the method, "Peel and dice one medium carrot. Cook").

Old historic cookbook recipes were pure lists of ingredients (2 carrots, 1 pound flour). They used roughly measured, basic, unprocessed ingredients and assumed a high level of cooking expertise on the part of the cook. Modern recipes often use preprocessed foodstuffs (e.g., canned soup stock) and offer much more help in the method. Modern recipes also give exact measurements and often a detailed, triple-tested scientific method.

Modern writers of cookbooks have to choose between a comprehensive and a simplified method of listing ingredients and method. A compromise will probably make sense to you.

(a) Comprehensive

In the old-fashioned, comprehensive method, ingredients and method are strictly separated. Ingredients may be roughly measured:

Ingredients:
　　1 carrot
　　1 potato
Method:
　　1. Peel and dice carrot and potato.
　　2. Steam vegetables about 5 minutes,
　　　　until fork tender. Drain and set aside to cool.
　　3. In large bowl combine carrots and potatoes.

Sample #10, Macaroni and cheese #5 (discussed in more detail below), uses a comprehensive method: readers are instructed in the method to shred the cheese called for in the ingredient list.

(b) Simplified

The modern style shortens and simplifies the method by including precooked, preprocessed ingredients:

Ingredients:
　　1 cup (250 mL) cooked diced carrots
　　1 cup (250 mL) cooked diced potatoes
Method:
　　1. In large bowl, combine carrots and potatoes.

Sample #6, Macaroni and cheese #1 (discussed in more detail below), uses a simplified method: the ingredient list calls for shredded cheese.

Whichever method you use, give instructions for finishing and serving that are helpful. Visual imagery may be necessary. It is often not enough to predict a cooking time, as in "Bake 30 minutes." It is much better to say, "Bake 30 minutes until golden or a toothpick comes out dry and crumb-free."

5. Yield

Describe the results in a way that is useful to readers ("Yields 2 cups [500 mL] or enough for 4 small servings"). Estimate servings on the basis of normal adult servings with appropriate accompanying side dishes.

This is also the place in the recipe to recommend or remind readers (if you previously mentioned this recommendation in the introduction) that doubling the recipe and freezing half or serving with a crumble of old cheddar works well with this dish.

The placement of this element in the recipe can vary, as you'll see in the sample recipes shown in this chapter. However, although the yield is sometimes found at the beginning of the recipe, it is more often the last element, given after the method.

d. Recipe styles

The technical side of recipe writing that is the recipe style may seem rigidly laid out, but it is not as rigid an exercise as you might think. Scanning the recipes of different cookbooks and magazines will give you insight into the many ways that recipes are written. Most list ingredients before method, but some don't. Some are long and detailed, some are short. There are many ways to write recipes, and in the end it does not really matter which recipe style you choose. What is important is that your recipes are clear about the ingredients and instruction, and that you are consistent from recipe to recipe throughout your book.

Before you write your book, you must determine your recipe style. You may exercise great creative license in the prose part of your text, but you owe it to your readers to include instructions for cooking that are straightforward and easy to understand. This calls for a consistent style.

If you are planning to submit your manuscript to publishers, you may want to check to see what recipe style the publishers you are targeting have used in other cookbooks and format your recipes in this style. Chapter 8 discusses publishing options and submitting to publishers in more detail.

1. Comparing recipe styles

A good way to decide which recipe style to use is to study other printed recipes in magazines and books. The larger magazines have their own style guidelines to which writers and editors scrupulously adhere. Larger book publishers also often have their own guidelines.

Samples #6 to #11 show six recipes for macaroni and cheese. Take a careful look at them and consider the style differences. (There is no right and wrong, just differences.) Notice the formatting. As you examine these samples, consider the following:

- How are the imperial and metric amounts presented?
- How much detail is given in the method?
- How much method (precooking or preparation) is given in the list of ingredients (simplified versus comprehensive method)?
- Are ingredients separated from method or integrated with the method?
- Are ingredients listed only once or listed as each ingredient is used?
- What kind of reader is each recipe written for?
- What level of competence is needed in the kitchen?
- Is the recipe set out in paragraph format or numbered steps?
- Does the format make a recipe more or less accessible to readers?
- Do you find any of the instructions confusing, the terms vague?
- Which recipe do you prefer? Why? Because it is easy to read? Easy to follow?
- Do you prefer the recipe with the author's personality in the anecdotal directions or the simple style?

2. Crafting your sentences

Although writing is discussed in more detail in later chapters, one thing worth considering at this stage is the way in which you are going to craft your sentences: will you begin each sentence of your instructions with a verb ("Combine in large bowl . . . ") or will you begin each instruction with the utensil ("In large bowl combine. . .")?

Sample #9 places utensils first, while the other recipe samples place verb first. Which do you find easier to read and follow?

Keep your style choice in mind as you continue the cookbook writing process.

3. How much detail?

Aim for clarity, consistency, and a balance between excruciating detail and none at all. Analyze your audience. How adept in the kitchen are your readers? Are you writing a book for children ("Ask your mother or father to set the oven to 350°F [180°C]. Be careful not to burn your fingers") or for experienced chefs ("Deglaze the pan")? How many home cooks would know how to deglaze a pan?

If your subject is ethnic cooking and calls for old-country methods uncommon in a modern kitchen, more explicit instructions are needed. Most of us would have trouble following the instructions, "Kraut your cabbage in a barrel." Most of us have neither oak barrels nor summer kitchens to provide optimum conditions for friendly bacteria to transform our cabbages.

Err on the side of too much detail rather than too little. Like any good teacher, you must not assume too much.

4. Timing is everything in cooking

Be consistent in your approach to timing throughout your book. Is it your aim to provide the best fare in the shortest amount of time or do you expect your readers to take the time and extra steps necessary to do something just so? You may have exceptions. For example, readers may be interested in recipes both for quick supper recipes and a complex, 17-step, wedding cake.

Don't homogenize or compress a recipe so it is unrecognizable just for consistency's sake. It would be preferable to omit the recipe entirely.

Using Checklist #1, check off the choices you have made for your recipe style. It doesn't matter which components you choose, but once chosen you should use them consistently throughout your book.

Bear in mind, though, that there are always practical exceptions. For example, do you always place instructions to preheat the oven at the beginning of the method? What do you do when a cooking

MACARONI AND CHEESE #1

metric		imperial
250 mL	elbow macaroni	1 cup
2 mL	basil	½ tsp.
2 mL	prepared mustard	½ tsp.
pinch	pepper	pinch
250 mL	shredded cheddar cheese	1 cup

*simplified method: cheese is
shredded in ingredient list*

Cook macaroni in lightly salted, boiling water according to package instructions. Drain. Stir in basil, mustard, and pepper; add cheese; mix lightly. Spoon into a 1.5 L (6 cup) casserole. Bake in a 180°C (350°F) oven 30 minutes until brown and bubbly.

Makes 4 servings.

MACARONI AND CHEESE #2 *(serves 4)*

unusual side-by-side format

1 cup (250 mL) elbow macaroni
½ tsp. (2 mL) basil
½ tsp. (2 mL) prepared mustard
Pinch pepper
1 cup (250 mL) shredded cheese

*preheat instructions
at beginning*

<u>Preheat</u> oven to 350°F (180°C).
Cook macaroni in lightly
salted, boiling water according
to package instructions.
Drain. Stir in basil, mustard, and
pepper; add cheese;
mix lightly. Spoon into a 6-cup
(1.5 L) casserole. Bake in a 350°F
(180°C) oven 30 minutes
until brown and bubbly.

little detail

MACARONI AND CHEESE #3

lists equipment separately

Ingredients:

1 cup (250 mL) macaroni
1 tsp. (5 mL) butter
½ tsp. (2 mL) basil
½ tsp. (2 mL) prepared mustard
Pepper to taste
1 cup (250 mL) grated cheddar cheese

Equipment:

Large pot
Colander
Measuring cup
Measuring spoon
1 large spoon
Casserole dish
(6 cup/1.5 L)

detailed method for inexperienced cook or child

aligned numbered steps

1. <u>Preheat</u> oven to 350°F (180°C).
2. <u>Bring</u> large pot of water to boil. Add macaroni, stir so it does not stick on bottom. In about 5 minutes, when macaroni is soft, dump into colander over sink. Run cold tap water through noodles. Drain well.
3. <u>Place</u> in buttered casserole. Stir in basil, mustard, pepper, and cheese.
4. <u>Bake</u> for 30 minutes until brown on top and bubbly. Use pot holders to remove from oven. Careful!

Makes enough for 4 to 6 people.

begins sentences with verb

MACARONI AND CHEESE #4

ingredient options

2 tablespoons (30 mL) <u>butter or margarine</u>
2 tablespoons (30 mL) all-purpose flour
¼ teaspoon (1 mL) salt
⅛ teaspoon (.5 mL) freshly ground black pepper
1 cup (250 mL) milk
½ cup (125 mL) grated sharp American cheese
½ cup (125 mL) grated Swiss cheese
½ teaspoon (2 mL) basil
½ teaspoon (2 mL) prepared mustard
1 cup (250 mL) cooked macaroni

begin sentence with utensil

integrated paragraph style with numbered steps

detailed method to educate curious reader

1. In <u>a heavy saucepan</u> melt butter or margarine over low heat. Blend in flour, salt, and pepper, stirring with a wooden spoon until no lumps remain. This is called a roux. 2. Add milk at once and stir constantly to evenly distribute the fat–flour mixture throughout the milk. 3. Cook over medium heat, stirring with a wooden spoon in figure-8 motions to evenly distribute the heat throughout the sauce. WARNING: DO NOT OVERBEAT. Over-zealous beating here will break down the starch into particles and make the mixture slick rather than velvety. 4. Continue cooking until bubbles appear across the whole surface. Thickening results when heat expands the starch particles in the flour. Cook 2 minutes more to make sure that the flour is cooked to remove the starchy taste. 5. Remove from heat and stir in cheeses, mustard, and basil. Pour over cooked macaroni and serve.

Makes dinner portions for 2 adults or 4 smaller servings.

MACARONI AND CHEESE #5

6 ounces (150 g) thin noodles
3 tablespoons (45 mL) buttter

3 tablespoons (45 mL) flour
¼ teaspoon (1 mL) salt

⅛ teaspoon (.5 mL) pepper
¼ pound (125 g) sharp
    Cheddar cheese
Paprika to garnish

comprehensive method:
cheese grated in method

paragraph
format

Cook noodles according to package; drain and pour into 2-quart (2 L) casserole dish. Melt butter, blend in flour, salt, and pepper; cook until bubbly. Slowly add milk. Cook until smooth and thickened, stirring constantly. Pour over noodles and sprinkle <u>grated cheese</u> on top. Cover and bake 45 minutes. Uncover, sprinkle with paprika, and place under broiler until brown and bubbly, approximately 3 minutes. <u>6 servings.</u>

yield included
in paragraph

*upscale
adaptation of
an old favorite*

FETTUCINE AND CHEESE #6

¼ pound (125 g) butter
¼ cup (50 mL) whipping cream
½ cup (100 mL) freshly grated aged Canadian cheddar cheese
¼ cup (50 mL) freshly grated imported Parmesan cheese
6 – 8 quarts (6 – 8 L) water
2 teaspoons (10 mL) salt
1 pound (500 g) homemade or commercial fresh fettucine

Cream the butter with a wooden spoon until light and fluffy and lemon-colored. Drip by drip, beat in the whipping cream. Beat in the cheeses. Cover the bowl and set aside.

*preheat instructions
in middle of recipe*

Preheat large casserole dish in 250°F (120°C) oven. Bring water and salt to a large rolling boil over high heat. Drop in fettucine and stir often to prevent strands from sticking together or to the pot. Continue to boil until soft but al dente. Avoid mushiness with a taste test — noodles should offer an ever-so-slight resistance to the bite. Drain fettucine in colander, gently throwing up in air to turn and drain excess water. Remove immediately to preheated casserole.

technical term

*fussy,
excruciating
detail*

Add butter, cream, and cheese mixture and toss to coat every strand evenly. Add salt and freshly ground pepper to taste. Serve at once. Enjoy!

4 servings.

method such as bread baking takes one-and-a-half hours before you need to place the dough in the oven? In this instance, you may put the oven temperature in the middle or at the end of the recipe. Be sure to add your own ideas to this list.

5. Format

The usefulness of a recipe depends to some extent on how it looks on the page, how easy it is to read. Pay attention to the different possibilities for alignment of ingredients and cooking instructions. Which format do you prefer? Do you have a better way of doing it? You'll be able to make some decisions as you compare with other cookbooks and as you work with your recipes. Different recipe styles will naturally lend themselves to certain formats. If you plan to place your cookbook with a publisher, you may wish to discuss your layout preference with the publisher.

Now that you have learned the secrets to clear recipe writing, have analyzed the different styles of recipes, and have considered which way you want to present yours, you are ready to move on to the next step of writing your cookbook — testing those recipes. Be sure to incorporate your style choices as you test, retest, and then edit the recipes.

❑ Introductions to all recipes
❑ Introductions to some recipes

❑ Metric measurement
❑ Imperial measurement
❑ Metric and imperial measurement

❑ List each ingredient only once
❑ List each ingredient as used

❑ Comprehensive food preparation method
❑ Simplified prepared ingredients method

❑ Comprehensive cooking method
❑ Simplified precooked ingredients method

❑ Lots of detail, help for reader
❑ Little detail, simplified as possible

❑ Begin sentence with verb
❑ Begin sentence with utensil

❑ Yield: at beginning
❑ Yield: at end

❑ Preheat instructions at beginning of recipe
❑ Oven temperature at end

Others:

_____
_____
_____
_____
_____
_____
_____
_____
_____
_____
_____
_____
_____
_____
_____

PART II
The Method

5
Preliminaries: scheduling and setting up your home office

a. Scheduling: creating a cookbook planning book

You will find yourself at different stages of the testing and writing process as work on your cookbook progresses. About to start a recipe, you discover someone has nibbled your last square of chocolate. You dash off to the grocery store to pick up a new box and run into an old friend. After a chat about your latest project, you are pleased to discover that she will be a terrific person to interview. So you set a date to see her. On the way home you stop by your editor's to pick up the recipes she has just finished editing for you. Add to that all the complexities of daily life: family, jobs, problems, and joys. Here are some organizational techniques to help you manage your work.

You are frazzled. You feel totally disorganized and behind. It's time to get out of the heat of the kitchen. Take yourself out to a quiet spot — the coffee shop on the corner or a spot by the river — take out your trusty planner and take control. Linger over an herbal tea and leaf through the pages, rearranging, scribbling down the odd comment, making a list, crossing off what you've accomplished. The planner is a graphic representation of your time and project. If it is well organized, you will be too.

1. Getting started

Visit a stationery store and buy a three-ring binder: a large one if you intend to plant it on your desk, a small one if you cannot go anywhere without it. Consider whether you will need large pages to make large sketches. Buy lots of dividers and divide your book project into sizable, manageable bits.

2. The front section

Keep general project timelines at the front section of your binder. Insert a calendar and fill in the major deadlines — an estimate of how many recipes have to be completed by a certain date. Write in some goals for yourself. Be realistic.

3. Recipe planning sections

Use the following suggestions as ideas for ways to organize your planning book:
(a) Ideas to be researched
(b) Recipes keyed into computer, ready for testing
(c) Tested recipes, ready for corrections on computer file
(d) Recipes ready for delivery to editor
(e) Recipes being edited
(f) Editor's corrections completed and returned, to be keyed in (editing of the recipes is discussed in further detail in chapter 7).

4. Names, addresses, and phone numbers

You will find that keeping a list of names, addresses, and phone numbers is useful as you write your book and also when it comes time to acknowledge people who helped you on the project. Include

Dozens of people will help you with your cookbook, and you will want to thank them in your book, send them a thank-you letter, or give them a gift copy of the book when it is out. Be sure to keep track of their names and addresses.

friends, colleagues, interviewees, and research librarians in your address list.

5. To-do lists

Lists are useful. As an alternative to those little scraps of paper next to the phone which disappear just when you need them, file your to-do lists safely in your binder. You'll then have only one place to look for them and you will get the satisfaction of crossing items off the list. Consider making daily, weekly, and monthly to-do lists.

b. Setting up a home office

Organize your paper. Buy a filing cabinet, folder, filing cards, steno pads, a daily planner, whatever it takes. If you don't, you'll end up with a heap of tomato-splotched scraps of paper. Put all your paper away in your office. This is important, even if the office is only a corner of the room. After all, you are a small business venture (see section **1.**).

Be sure to file your electronic data properly too.

1. Expenses

Between the trips to the store, stocking the shelves with ingredients, researching, testing, and retesting, expenses and their paper records will pile up. Standard office procedures will help you keep this in line. Be methodical and businesslike. It's important to file paper properly. Collecting receipts on the kitchen table will not do. Keep a separate file folder of invoices, grocery receipts, and any other expense receipts you accumulate from your cookbook project.

Keep track of all your expenses that may be useful for tax purposes. If you are a self-employed writer you are entitled to declare expenses that you must expend in order to earn money. You are, after all, a small business and a professional. If the cookbook is a community or organization's project, the organization may also be able to claim certain expenses. Government pamphlets will give you guidelines, but seek professional tax advice, especially if you are building a cottage industry around your cookbook by publishing it yourself.

Keep track of your business expenses such as:
- Telephone bills for all your long distance calls related to selling, researching, interviewing, and promoting your book

Prioritize your to-do lists:

U = urgent

E = easy

W = can wait

Keep track of all your
long distance phone
calls in your scheduling
binder. It will make
separation of personal
from business phone
use easier when tax
time comes.

- Office supplies: paper, printer ink, paper clips, stamps, stationery, steno pads
- Gas for your vehicle or other transportation expenses
- Printing costs: photocopies
- Writer's equipment: computer and software, tape recorder
- Books for your professional library
- Ingredients for testing recipes
- Equipment purchased specifically to enable you to taste recipes (depending on how much it is used for personal versus business use): pots, pans, etc.

2. Planning

If you itemize your invoices and receipts in a list, you can then use the list to plan. For example, you may want to analyze how much groceries are costing you. If you are self-publishing (chapter 8 discusses self-publishing in more detail), you will need to factor this into your retail price. If you are working with a publisher, you may have to account for your expenses if you haven't negotiated a flat fee for testing expenses.

6
Testing,
testing . . .

If you publish untested recipes, prepare yourself for some pretty ugly mail! Recipes must always be tested at least once, and more than once if possible. It would be unfair to readers who have invested considerable money and time in a recipe to have it flop because of an improper pan size or cooking time. Even tried-and-true recipes should be retested if they are written in a new style, as a subtle difference in instructions can create different results. Magazines brag that they have triple-tested their recipes, but very few home testers can afford to test more than once. As anyone who has followed a recipe can testify, though, even with these guarantees, variations occur due to temperature, air pressures, or the temperament of the cook.

Chances are your test kitchen is none other than your very own messy but much-loved home kitchen. Your test range is not gleaming stainless but blueberry-stained enamel. Very few of us can afford a real home economist's lab. That's okay. It will be a reality check to have your kids "yucking" over certain dishes and your neighbors dropping by for coffee and coffee cake on which you need a frank opinion. Many introductions to cookbooks extol the virtues of families who have virtuously eaten their way through mountains of potatoes and vats of sauerkraut.

But the reality is that you have a lot of real work ahead of you, work that must be fitted into an already full day. Every writer has a unique life situation. Are you writing your book on weekends and evenings after a long day at work? Is it a summer project or a lifelong collection? Are you testing recipes with a crying baby in the room or an efficient assistant? In spite of the differences, everyone writing a cookbook has a similar challenge. It can feel a bit overwhelming at times unless you are organized when you approach it.

If you are writing a community cookbook, forming a testing committee usually works best. It will allow the work of testing to be spread amongst members. You may want to review section **b.2.** in chapter 2 on recipe testing with a committee.

a. Analyzing your testing time

Let's say that either you or the publisher has decided that your book should include 125 recipes. How do you estimate the time involved? Multiply the number of hours you estimate it will take to make each recipe by the number of recipes: 125 recipes x 1 hour = 125 hours. Sample #12 shows a sample analysis of the time required to test a recipe. Use Worksheet #8 to analyze the time it takes you to test your recipes.

Your estimate amounts to a good guess, at best. I've learnt from experience that it is almost impossible to come up with a scientific formula for a testing time analysis. But as you become more experienced at testing, you'll find that your estimates become more and more accurate.

You may have noticed that the time taken if you encounter a problem with a recipe is not factored into this equation. You may want to add a 10% margin to your time analysis to cover any unforeseen problems. Section **d.4.** below discusses troubleshooting recipes.

b. Before you begin testing: setting up your test kitchen

There are a number of things you can do to make your testing more efficient.

Sample #12
Recipe test time analysis

Title of recipe: _____ Macaroni and cheese _____

Shopping: _____ 5 minutes (portion of 45 minutes spent in store) _____

Keying in recipe: _____ 20 minutes _____

Noncooking preparation time: _ 10 minutes _____

_____ (getting ingredients out and measured, grating cheese) ___

Cooking time: _____ 10 minutes (making white sauce, cooking and draining _____

_____ noodles, buttering pan, mixing bread crumb topping) _____

Editing recipe on screen: _____ 5 minutes _____

Total time: _____ 50 minutes _____

Worksheet #8
Recipe test time analysis

Title of recipe: _____

Shopping: _____

Keying in recipe: _____

Noncooking preparation time: _____

_____

Cooking time: _____

_____

Editing recipe on screen: _____

Total time: _____

- Calibrate your oven thermometer. You may be surprised at the inaccuracy of the dial. Fifty degrees doesn't make much difference in everyday cooking, but you don't want to get hate mail about burnt buns. As a double check, get an inexpensive oven thermometer for reassurance.

- Invest in proper ingredient measuring tools: measuring cups and spoons, and thermometers for meat and candy, for starters. As an experienced cook, you probably have gained a degree of confidence in measuring and cooking by instinct — a handful of this and that. The challenge will be to get the facts down. Exactly how much flour? Recipes must be precise. "Allow bread to rise until it feels right" is not good enough for a beginning baker.

- Buy a good quality timer. It will prove invaluable. Digital timers allow you to count down the seconds easily.

- Invest in kitchen appliances and gadgets, but don't go wild unless you can afford them. These may be legitimate business expenses, but it's best to consult a tax accountant before assuming they are.

- Use kitchen tools that will be present in your readers' kitchens. Are you writing a self-help nutrition guide for low-income young mothers and toddlers? Don't include recipes that can be made only in expensive breadmakers. You can, however, assume that few cooks today would attempt to make a cake without an electric mixer.

In the process of testing, you will be stopping to pick up pencil and paper to make a comment, change a time, alter a process. Be disciplined about making notes, either on hardcopy or directly on the computer file, while it is all fresh in your mind. If not, you may end up having to retest a recipe.

c. Secrets of efficient recipe testing

Before you begin the process of developing your recipes, review these tips. They will help make recipe testing as efficient as possible.

- Integrate recipes into regular meal times as much as possible. As long as you're cooking, you might as well feed your family — unless of course they don't enjoy sautéed calamari.

- Make testing as much fun as possible. Consider each recipe a challenge, a scientific experiment. After all, you are writing a cookbook because you like to cook, remember?

- Don't name something until it's finished. No one will know the delicious soup in your book is actually watery stew gone awry.

- Give results away. Find single friends or anyone else you know who would appreciate a home-cooked meal and the excitement of being a "tester" for a book.

- Groceries:

  ° Prepare detailed grocery lists.

  ° Economize on time by shopping for batches of recipes at a time.

  ° Keep shopping for test ingredients completely separate from family groceries: in your mind, on recipe lists, in grocery carts, on your kitchen shelves. If you don't, you will inevitably find yourself in the middle of an expensive test when you run out of something.

One of the most important things to remember is to always be protective of your time and privacy. Unplug the telephone while testing sensitive dishes such as those involving chocolate. As everyone who runs a home-based business knows, friends think you are fair game because you're home answering the phone or doorbell. Be polite but firm. When there is no clear distinction between work and home, people don't understand your need for uninterrupted time. Ten minutes of gossip goes by in what seems to be a minute, but it only takes a minute to burn a pie crust.

d. Developing recipes

There are six major steps in developing a recipe.

1. Step one: first draft

Once you have the recipe, whether it has been transposed from a book or is from a friend or other source, write it down. Better still, key it into your computer, if you have one, in the recipe style you have chosen to use for your book. With testing, anything can be altered: ingredients, method, timing. But once the first draft is down, you have a starting point, something to work on and perfect. Changes will be only a few keystrokes away.

Six steps to developing

a recipe:

1. First draft

2. Kitchen test

3. Taste test

4. Retest

5. Computer edit

6. Enhancement

2. Step two: kitchen test

Once you have written down the recipe or input it on your computer, take your rough draft recipe to the kitchen. Read your instructions and prepare the dish, making changes in pencil in the margins, as needed. Write notes to yourself right on the recipe: "too soggy, try less milk," or "retest at 375°F/190°C."

Timing is hard to predict, so write down the minimum time you think the recipe needs, for example, 45 minutes for a cake. As it becomes obvious that the cake needs another 5 minutes, reset the timer and add +5 to the draft recipe. Add as many +5s as necessary, then add up the time once you have finished preparing the dish.

3. Step three: taste test

The taste test is a very important step. Get as many objective opinions as possible. Set up formal tastings with fill-in questionnaires, drop samples off with neighbors, or grab the kids as they run through the kitchen. Whenever possible, try out your recipes on the kinds of people who will buy your book. Try the Cookie Cutter Zoo Sandwiches at a preschool birthday party. Are the kids delighted? Deliver the mushy pea bisque to the senior citizens for their opinion. Is it spicy enough for them? Too spicy?

Although you should have no trouble finding friends and family to try your culinary experiments, treat them well or after a while they will start to complain that they are being treated like guinea pigs. Remember that taste is very subjective. Here are a few guidelines for a taste test. Ask your tasters to answer the following questions either informally, by chatting with you, or formally on a questionnaire you have created based on the following questions:

(a) *Appearance:* Is the dish appetizing? Are the colors appealing? Would using different-colored ingredients improve the dish?

(b) *Presentation:* Would the dish look better with a garnish or a sauce?

(c) *Flavor:* Do you like the overall flavor? Is it spicy, salty, sweet, or sour enough for your taste? What would you do to make it better? Does one ingredient overwhelm the others?

(d) *Texture:* How would you describe the texture? Does it suit the dish? Do the ingredients seem overcooked? Are there textural contrasts? How would you improve the texture?

The taste test — five characteristics to analyze:

1. Appearance
2. Presentation
3. Flavor
4. Texture
5. Aroma

(e) *Aroma:* Does the dish smell appetizing? Is it too strong or not strong enough?

4. Step four: retest if necessary

If you are not content with the results of the recipe or you want to try incorporating any suggestions and criticisms you gained from the taste tests that you think might be valid, now is the time to retest the recipe.

Retest the recipe however many times it takes you to get it right. Be sure to correct your draft recipe as well.

Some things will go wrong in spite of your best efforts. Make changes and try, try again. The following tips suggest various elements you might try modifying in the recipe if it wasn't quite right the first time:

- Try substituting different ingredients
- Try adding ingredients, spices, and flavors
- Try substituting different amounts of ingredients
- Try precooking or preparing ingredients differently
- Try changing the order of the method of the recipe
- Try cooking or baking at a lower or higher temperature
- Try changing the cooking or baking time
- Try a microwave or a conventional oven

5. Step five: computer edit

Once you have had received feedback from the taste tests and have retested, incorporating any changes, return to the computer and alter your recipe to reflect any changes you will make. Print out the revised recipe, but keep your smudged original kitchen notes. If you make a typographical error, you may have to refer back to them.

If you do not have a computer, use a friend's computer or ask a friend to help you. There are also many students who would be happy to earn a bit of money at this small job. Ask at the local school.

6. Enhancing the usefulness of your recipes

Always be aware of additional information you can give readers that will enhance the usefulness of your recipes. This information can be included in the recipe introduction, in a note at the end of the recipe, or in a sidebar to the recipe. Here are some ideas:

- Shopping lists

Always keep your smudged original kitchen notes, even after you have printed out the fresh, revised recipe. If you make a typographical error, you may have to refer back to them.

- Work plan (i.e., mention if you can start preparing the dish the day before, the night before, or early in the day)
- Nutritional information
- Consumer advice: where to buy ingredients
- Historical, botanical background of ingredients
- Storage advice
- Cost of ingredients
- Serving suggestions
- Menu accompaniments
- Garnishes
- Dietary substitutions
- Altitude conversions
- Equipment needed
- Glossary of terms
- Alternative cooking methods (e.g., microwave, stovetop, oven method)
- Leftovers
- Recipe enhancers (e.g., how to steam carrots when the recipe calls for "cooked carrots")
- An appropriate wine
- Variations (dried herb for fresh)

e. Don't be afraid to give readers warnings

When writing your recipes, it's usually best to phrase things in a positive way. But occasionally an oddball comment can be really helpful. For example, making fudge can be tricky even with a candy thermometer. There's a stage between soft and runny and hard and crystalline which can last 1 minute or 20 minutes, depending on the temperature of the room. A cautionary note would help, such as, "Watch out! Fudge is tricky! As you stir, watch for resistance of the mixture on the wooden spoon. As soon as it becomes a chore to stir, working quickly, scoop into buttered pan." This type of advice is especially useful to cooks who are venturing into new, challenging territory.

If you want to write a flambé cookbook full of combustibles and flames, by all means, do it. But remember to add lively disclaimers

(WARNING, BE CAREFUL), and add detailed instructions, lots of do's and don'ts. The same type of warning is necessary in barbecue cookbooks, and even cookbooks that do not involve danger except for readers of a certain age.

f. What if a recipe flops?

It can be a disappointing waste of time, money, and energy if a dish you make flops. It may be worth fiddling with the recipe or not. But don't be afraid to cut your losses. You'll probably learn something from the experience, if only what not to do. Every business suffers waste and loss. Treat it as a variable to be realistically factored into your costs and timing.

Before you decide to throw out a recipe, consider whether it is worthwhile to do a bit of troubleshooting. The tips offered in section **d.4.** above on troubleshooting may help salvage a recipe.

Never be tempted to include a recipe in which you do not have total confidence. If you do, it will come back later as self-doubt when you are promoting your book. Still worse, you may hear from an angry reader whose birthday cake was ruined by your recipe for runny icing.

This doesn't mean that you have to like the taste of every recipe in your cookbook . . . as long as somebody does.

There are all kinds of reasons for including a recipe your tasters — including yourself — give mixed reviews. Writing a book about family traditions, you may interview an 80-year-old Italian matron with a poignant childhood memory of her father's spaghetti with anchovy and black olive sauce which he prepared every Christmas Eve. Your children protest that they prefer pizza pops to real Italian. When writing the recipe, give options to reduce the salty fish taste, but definitely include the original with a wonderful introduction about your Italian contact. Chances are you'll get a nice note from a reader who has been searching high and low for this dish: her great-grandmother used to make it.

Now that you've selected and tested the recipes you will include in your cookbook, the real work of writing begins. This is your chance not only to develop your writing skills but also to inspire your readers to try your recipes and share your love of food.

7
Writing about food

Ask your friends who have dozens of cookbooks on their bookshelves if they've tried many of the recipes from these books, and they inevitably respond with a sheepish, "Well, no," but then enthusiastically add, "but I do read them just for fun."

What is it about cookbooks that makes people want to read them? They're tremendously entertaining when created by good writers and illustrators whose work is enhanced by good book designers. You'll produce a much better cookbook if you offer readers more than a list of cooking instructions. Why not become a food writer?

Food writing is writing just like any other kind of writing. The subject is food, a subject so basic to human experience that food writing is found extensively and universally, everywhere from canned bean labels to Pulitzer Prize novels, on menus and advertisements, in newspapers and magazines, in books and on the World Wide Web.

Writings about food cover everything from the philosophy of food, food's religious importance, its social value, and its influence on language, to the scientific and technical aspects of food, including agriculture and the culinary arts. Scholarly dialogue debates the role of food in literature, history, geography, cultural anthropology, and biography.

The food industry is huge and diverse. Facets of the food community include culinary professionals, growers, manufacturers, vintners, marketers, chefs, restaurateurs, food writers, editors, publishers, broadcasters, academics, researchers, food scientists, nutritionists, home economists, educators, caterers, retailers and suppliers, ad companies, and copy writers. Each is an expert in his or her own right and an invaluable source for your research. He or she may also be a market for your book.

With all these perspectives to choose from, how you approach your topic, what you choose to communicate on the subject of food, is up to you.

There is a natural logical flow to writing. You start with a curiosity, a need to know. You set out to find answers, talk to people, and read a lot. Then you sit down with pad and paper or in front of a blank computer screen. Entering a semimeditative state, your brain starts to integrate what you've learned with what you already know. You make mental connections and generate images, which you transcribe into words in the material world. Stepping away from your work for a break, you later return and change some of the words around. Then you pass it to someone else to look it over.

The four logical steps of writing are —

> (a) researching printed materials,
>
> (b) interviewing,
>
> (c) writing, and
>
> (d) editing.

You may want to review section **c.1.** in chapter 3 on copyright before you begin your research and interviewing.

a. Step one: research

All writers, no matter in what genre of writing, from fairy tales to literary criticism, have one thing in common: they research their subjects. Conducting research for a cookbook is the same as researching any other book. As a curious person, you seek out every possible source of information on your topic through reading and interviewing. Your passing interests evolve into a passionate need to know.

The subject of food is a subject so basic to human experience that it is found extensively and universally, everywhere from canned bean labels to Pulitzer Prize novels.

In the beginning you have just the abstract concept that interested a publisher or fuels you in your choice of self-publishing. Your end product, your book, will inevitably be different than you initially imagined (although it can't be too different if you have an agreement with a publisher for a certain type of book). This can be an exciting process and research is an important part of it. It's best to be open-minded.

Your topic may appear to be simple: an apple cookbook. But you discover a myriad of directions in which you can go and dozens of questions. Is there a difference between a cooking apple and a noncooking apple? What is the best pie apple? Are green apples more nutritious than red ones? Is the story of Johnny Appleseed true? What are the best soil conditions for apple trees? What is the natural history of the apple? How many different varieties are there?

You set out for an agricultural library at the local university where out-of-print volumes list historic varieties.

Using Worksheet #9, begin researching your subject. Write a paragraph defining your subject on the worksheet. This is your starting point. Then, write out a series of questions about the subject. Next, identify and underline key search words in these questions, listing the words on the chart. Look up key words in a dictionary and write out definitions on the worksheet. Underline the key search words in the definitions. These key search words will guide you as you look through the following resources:

(a) Encyclopedias. Look up key words in the index to the volumes.

(b) Library card catalogue. Look up these words in the subject drawers of the catalogue.

(c) Computer catalogue. Key your search words into the word search field.

(d) Periodicals, magazines, and journals. *Reader's Guide to Periodical Literature* and *Canadian Periodical Index* are good places to begin your search. Ask the librarian for other subject indexes. If the index is in book form, search by subject. If on a database, do a word search.

(e) World Wide Web and the Internet. Use any search engine and key in your key search words. Then try another search engine. You'll likely find that no single engine will satisfy all your search needs.

Subject: (Write a paragraph.)

_____
_____
_____
_____
_____
_____
_____
_____

Questions on this subject:

1. _____
_____
_____
_____

2. _____
_____
_____
_____

3. _____
_____
_____
_____

4. _____
_____
_____
_____

5. _____
_____
_____
_____

Key search word: Definition:

_____   _____
_____   _____
_____   _____
_____   _____
_____   _____
_____   _____
_____   _____
_____   _____
_____   _____
_____   _____
_____   _____
_____   _____
_____   _____
_____   _____
_____   _____
_____   _____
_____   _____
_____   _____
_____   _____

If you reach a dead end, scan the table of contents of several of the books you have found. You will find fresh approaches to your research topic and new key words or places to start.

As you uncover more details, be sure to write down notes, perhaps keeping a separate page for each topic and subtopic. Don't forget to record the book, magazine, Web site, person, or other source the information is from. You never know when you'll need to refer back to it to doublecheck a cryptic or illegible notation. The background material you have uncovered through your research will be useful when you come to write the introductions to the various chapters and sections of your book.

b. Step two: interviewing

Now you've done your solid research into written sources and wonder, why bother with live interviews? Because a face-to-face communication can inspire you. Talk to someone who is excited about a topic and it may just give you the jolt you need to make your writing come alive. You merely have to collect the quotes that will jump off the page. Consider the vast wealth of knowledge that exists in the minds of people who never write a word. Would you want to deprive yourself of that?

Now you just need to determine who to interview.

1. Interview experts

Interview chefs and restaurateurs, experts in the government, and especially marketing and agriculture experts who can put you in touch with other experts like growers and manufacturers. They are all in the business of promoting their products so they have lots of printed materials. Some translate scientific information (such as technical papers on the different varieties of potato) into lay language. Often they have excellent recipes and don't mind sharing them.

But you don't have to stick to subjects related only to your expert's area of expertise. Interviewing an orchardist? Ask not only his or her opinion on growing practices but also more subjective questions. What is the orchardist's favorite apple variety and why? Which apple makes the best pie?

2. Interview nonexperts

People all around you have a wealth of cooking and recipe knowledge. A neighbor may remember how his East Indian grandmother made a perfect parantha, combining just the right amount of oil and cold butter. Your friend who went on Sunday clam digs with her family would know more about how to steambake a clam in seaweed over a bonfire than any bivalve biologist at a city university.

As mentioned earlier in chapter 2, both personal and historical anecdotes are often an important part of community cookbooks. Keep this in mind as you research and write your material. The exciting thing about food writing is that it gives you the opportunity to capture snippets of living culture that come only from firsthand sources.

3. Interviewing guidelines

The following are some guidelines for conducting interviews but, as always, there are exceptions. It's a good idea to be prepared for an interview with a list of questions, but you should also be prepared to set aside that list if something more relevant comes up during the discussion. If you know the kind of information you want, you will be better at extracting it from your interviewee and keeping on topic. But in doing so, you may also impose your own ideas and personality on the person you are interviewing and miss out on something quite different, perhaps, wonderful. The objective of any interview, and any conversation, is honest communication involving give and take. The challenge is to strike a balance, to offer your sincere interest without overwhelming the other person.

You'll find that most people are happy to give you interviews. It's more likely that they'll want to talk longer than you have time for or give you more information than you need. Be firm and polite. You don't want to disappoint someone by writing only a few lines after talking with them for four hours. After a while, you will develop a sense about how much time you need to acquire the required information.

- Face-to-face interviews are ideal, but time, distance, and money constraints make telephone and e-mail interviews a good compromise.

- When contacting someone for an interview, do not assume that they have time to talk to you on the spot. Arrange to call them back at a convenient time. Give them a general idea about the subject matter you will be discussing.

It's a good idea to be prepared for an interview with a list of questions, but you should also be prepared to set aside that list if something more relevant comes up during the discussion.

*Number the pages
of your notes in
advance to avoid
the scramble later.*

- Prepare a list of questions to ask during the interview. You may deviate from the topic, but it's a starting point to return to if you get off track.

- Prepare adequate writing materials: lots of pens and pencils, a steno pad, or whatever you feel most comfortable using. Number pages in advance to avoid the scramble later.

- If your notes are barely legible, transpose them to your computer as soon as possible. You may not be able to read them one week later.

- Be very careful transposing recipes. A slip of the pen and one teaspoon becomes one tablespoon. Ask your subject to repeat measurements, and read back what you have written if you are unsure about something. Suggest specific amounts and methods if descriptions are vague. You can clean this up during testing and re-writing.

- Ask your subject to spell out names and places and to repeat dates.

- Quotations make your writing come alive, so develop a sense, an ear for what looks good in print. Do this by analyzing the work of others. In the meantime, catch as many interesting quotes as possible.

*Ask your subject
to repeat
measurements,
and read back
what you have
written if you are
unsure about
something.*

Should you use handwritten notes or a tape recorder? It's your call. You may want to use both methods of taking notes, as they are both excellent in different ways. The machine is better than your brain for catching exact quotes, but it can't jot down impressions or make editorial comments. You may make observations that would be rude to record on tape in front of someone (e.g., wildly moving hands while explaining the perfect tomato sauce). Occasionally a comment you make in your notes becomes the lead sentence to the piece you are writing.

A tape recorder may also inhibit the person you are interviewing. Reassure them that the tape is for your ears only, to jog your memory (that is, unless you plan to use the interview on the radio; if you do, let your interviewee know).

Scanning a page of notes from a one-hour interview may take a few minutes, but listening to a one-hour interview on tape takes exactly one hour. Editing tape can be very boring, but if you rely on accurate details and exact wording and even sounds in the room, an audiotape is a useful tool.

4. Interviewing family

If you are writing a biographical cookbook, you will stir up memories, both good and bad, so be sensitive to the situation. Consider Christmas, often a bittersweet experience. It's a time for family to reunite and celebrate, yet many people find themselves overwhelmed by all the activity.

Interviewing more than one member of a family at a time can be a mixed blessing depending on the family chemistry. One person may help jog the other's memory, but he or she may also constantly interrupt and overshadow the other member of the family, causing you to lose all of the other person's insights. You must maintain control of the interview.

c. Step three: writing

Food writing both informs and entertains. Sometimes it does more. It educates and transmits cultural values by relating "This is the way I cook, how I feel about food, how we have cooked for generations."

1. Avoid hackneyed writing

Bad food writing is bossy and insincere, vague and full of clichés. Lazy food writers rely on a boring rehash of words and phrases. Here are a few of them; make a point not to use them.

- Cool and clear
- Delicate aroma
- Delicious and nutritious
- Delight the palate
- Fancy dishes
- Fine dining
- Fine flavor
- Fit for a king
- Flavorsome
- From scratch
- Full-bodied flavor
- Garden fresh
- Healthful hints
- Hot and spicy
- Lip-smacking
- Mouth-watering
- Pleasing to the taste
- Sink your teeth into
- Stick to your ribs
- Sweet and succulent
- Tantalizingly
- Taste sensation
- Taste tempting
- Tasty treat
- Tender morsels
- Tickle the taste buds
- Tickle the tummy

Try to avoid using the expression "cooking from scratch." It conjures up all kinds of unappetizing images!

Look to texture to define what makes the difference between mundane and sophisticated cooking.

Don't use the word "smell" to describe the fragrance that fills a room when cinnamon buns are baking. It looks bad in print. You might as well say "the buns stunk good." As well, avoid "food porn" — expressions such as "sinfully delicious," "orgasmic chocolate," and "lusty lasagna."

2. Make your food writing sparkle

Good food writing, on the other hand, is alive with vibrant words and images. Powerful feelings flow through good writing. It is grounded in clear, intelligent thought.

Words such as caramel, crunch, crispy, and crackling are appetizing to look at. Use onomatopoeia to describe food. Children have an acute sensitivity to texture, so look to them for inspiration. Of course, use these terms appropriately.

Always try to put a positive spin on things. Don't describe fish as fishy, gluey, slimy, gelatinous, oily. It is rich, moist, smooth, flaky.

Good food writing is far more than a literal description of food. Bring all that you are to your writing — your own experience, insights, poignant memories, and intelligence. This doesn't mean that your writing has to be personal unless you choose to put yourself into your work. It is possible to write with warmth without using the words "I" or "we." It's up to you (possibly with the help of an editor) to find a voice and a distance from your writing that feels natural and comfortable.

The fragrance of food

Earthy	Fruity	Musky
Flowery	Heady	Spicy

The sound of food

Bubbling	Gurgle	Slosh
Burble	Pop	Swish
Crackle	Rasp	Tinkle
Crunch	Rustle	Whir
Fizzle	Sizzle	Whistle

Good food writing evokes emotions. Consider the nostalgic attachment that people have for chocolate chip cookies. Think of Christmas, the vision of a golden stuffed turkey, mashed potatoes, jeweled cranberry sauce, and a feeling of family. Evoke these emotions in your writing.

Good food writing also recreates the physical and experiential. All five senses — taste, smell, sound, touch, and sight — are used in eating; they should be used in food writing, too. Your food images

The touch and texture of food

Brittle	Diluted	Leathery	Sandy
Bubbly	Doughy	Mashed	Shredded
Buoyant	Dry	Massaged	Silky
Caressed	Fluffy	Pasty	Soft
Chewy	Frothy	Pithy	Solid
Congealed	Gelatinous	Pliant	Spongy
Crisp	Grainy	Powdery	Squishy
Crumbly	Grated	Pressed	Stiff
Curdled	Gritty	Pulpy	Supple
Delicate	Jellied	Rolled	Tender
Dense	Kneaded	Rubbed	Watery

The sight of food

Blush	Flaky	Matte	Speckled
Bright	Flecked	Milky	Sprinkled
Clear	Flushed	Mottled	Steamy
Colored	Frosted	Pale	Stippled
Creamy	Glossy	Peppered	Studded
Dappled	Glowing	Sheen	Tinted
Faded	Lackluster	Shiny	Translucent

The taste of food

Acidic	Flat	Overripe	Sugary
Astringent	Full-bodied	Piquant	Sweet
Biting	Gamy	Racy	Tangy
Bittersweet	Honeyed	Salty	Tart
Briny	Juicy	Savory	Tinny
Brisk	Metallic	Sharp	Vinegary
Candied	Mild	Spicy	Weak
Fermented	Moist	Stinging	Zesty
Fiery	Nippy	Succulent	Zippy

should jump off the page, especially in the recipe introductions where you want to entice readers to try a dish.

How do you convey the creaminess of chocolate pudding, the snap of freshly harvested carrots, the heady fragrance of plum pudding steaming up the kitchen, the vision of a bakery window festooned with Christmas stollen and gingerbread men, chocolate truffles dusted with confectionery sugar, a gingerbread house plastered with jujubes and honey crisps, chocolate kisses and peppermint sticks?

Of all the senses involved in eating, taste, the most prominent, is ironically the most difficult to describe. Often we describe one taste by comparing it to another. Apples taste like pears, like pineapples. Try conjuring up an image of the taste of cinnamon. It tastes like, well, cinnamon.

Good food writing creates a spiritual connection between people and food. Food is valued for far more than its ability to abate hunger. Food is part of the tapestry of culture. Consider food taboos and eating trends today, such as vegetarianism amongst an environmentally conscious younger generation. Consider the healing qualities of chicken soup.

And finally, good food writing involves the intellect. Write for readers' curiosity. Many books and magazines combine geography and travel, history and gardening, with recipes. Methodical research is essential.

Good food writing . . .

- evokes emotions

- recreates the physical and experiential

- creates a spiritual connection between people and food

- involves the intellect

Beginning writers often make the mistake of believing that they must be totally self-sufficient when they sit down to write, that all inspiration, all words, must spring forth spontaneously or else they are cheating. What you bring to your work is a desire to write, a need to communicate. You may even know what you want to say. Saying it is another story. For some writers, words flow easily. For others, every single word committed to the page is torture. The challenge is in coming up with the words. It is easy to be overwhelmed by emotions or confused by too much data and to be at a loss for words. Help is on the way.

It is wise for a beginning writer to invest in a good general dictionary, a thesaurus, and a writer's style book. I recommend a *Roget's Thesaurus* based on the old 1852 edition where the words and phrases are listed in categories according to their meaning or logical connections. It leads you to new ideas you didn't even realize were there. Looking for the name of a particular cheese you ate on a trip to Europe last summer? Roget lists the names of about 275 cheeses from Aettekees to Wisconsin. As well, there are all kinds of writing and style books in the market (several are listed in the bibliography at the end of this book). Invest in a few.

3. *How much should you write without a publishing contract?*

How much of the book you write before you have an agreement from a publisher to publish your book depends entirely on you. If you're an unpublished beginner, you will need to prove to yourself and any prospective publisher that you can write. It wouldn't hurt to write two or three chapters to see if your thesis or concept holds. Do you really have a fresh approach and new ideas and recipes? What is so special and different about your book? Once you have written a couple of chapters, ask a friend you really trust to edit it and then get his or her feedback on your project.

Of course, if you plan to self-publish your book, this question isn't really relevant — you will need all of the material written before you proceed. However, you may still want to have a trustworthy friend read a couple of chapters you have written and then get his or her feedback on your project.

Chapter 8 discusses both trade publishing (with a publisher) and self-publishing in more detail.

Writer's tools:

- Dictionary
- Thesaurus
- Writer's style book

d. Step four: editing

You may edit your own work, but often it is better to find someone with an objective eye to do it. You might want to consider hiring a professional editor if you are self-publishing. Working with an editor is discussed in section **4.** below.

1. Editing your work

Writers before the days of computers would simply put pen to paper and cover it with words. The writing process was recognized by the number of crumpled pieces of paper, or drafts, in the waste basket. Today we write with computers, effortlessly cutting and pasting electronic blips on the screen. Writing is more about intuitive merging and deletion than mechanical crumpling.

Very few people get down their thoughts and message word-for-word perfect the first time. Some writers relish the spontaneous flush as words first spring to mind and screen. Others find a first draft to be pure agony, much preferring the fiddling stage, the self-edit.

Today with computers, fancy fonts, and laser printing, material tends to look good long before it is ready for publication. And there is a whole new generation of computer-generated typographical errors to correct: sloppy pastes and half-changed tenses. It's hard to track your own writing process. Be patient. Take at least an overnight break between drafts. Some writers edit on the screen. Others print out drafts on paper and edit with a pencil before making corrections on the screen.

If you are editing your own work, remember that consistency is all important; the edit must ensure that each recipe follows the recipe style guidelines you have chosen. Use Checklist #2 to ensure that all areas are considered. Alter or add to the form to suit your needs.

If your book is aimed at an inexperienced cook, find friends who are not confident in the kitchen to see if the recipes make sense to them. Better still, have your friends try out the recipes by making a few of the dishes.

Chapter 6 discusses the editing process that is involved in testing the recipes, so you will have already done much of this work. However, it never hurts to test a recipe one last time or at least read it through to ensure clarity and consistency. Appendix 2 will help you make conversions between metric and imperial measurements.

Remember that consistency is all important; the edit must ensure that each recipe follows the recipe style guidelines you have chosen.

Checklist #2
Editing a recipe

Recipe: _____

Date: _____

Title:

❑ Clearly communicates what is being prepared

❑ If not, suggested alternative_____

_____

_____

Introduction:

❑ Enhances the recipe

❑ Is irrelevant to the recipe

❑ If irrelevant, suggested alternative_____

_____

_____

List of ingredients:

❑ Metric units used

❑ Imperial units used

❑ Consistent blend of metric and imperial

❑ If both used: conversions are accurate

❑ Conversion corrections completed on copy

❑ Ingredients listed in order used in method

❑ All ingredients listed and matching in list and method

Checklist #2 — Continued

<u>**Instructions/method:**</u> (Personalize this list with items from Checklist #1.)

- ❑ Logical steps used and in order
- ❑ Consistency in terminology
- ❑ Comprehensive food preparation method used
- ❑ Simplified prepared ingredients method used
- ❑ Comprehensive cooking method used
- ❑ Simplified precooked ingredients method used
- ❑ Consistently begins with verb
- ❑ Consistently begins with utensil
- ❑ Yield at beginning
- ❑ Yield at end
- ❑ Preheat instructions at beginning
- ❑ Oven temperature at end
- ❑ Temperatures added to copy
- ❑ Time given seems reasonable
- ❑ Time given seems unreasonable

Other: _____

_____

_____

<u>**General:**</u>

- ❑ Recipe can be shortened
- ❑ Standard terminology used

Suggestions for improvement: _____

_____

_____

2. Structural editing

(a) Parts of a book

Now is the time to make sure you've got all the bits and pieces that make up a book. The easiest way to determine the final structure of your book is to analyze your favorite cookbooks. How are they structured? What book components do they include? The standard elements are listed below. You may choose to incorporate all these components, or only some of them.

(a) Title page

(b) Copyright page

(c) Dedication

(d) Table of contents

(e) Foreword

(f) Preface

(g) Acknowledgments

(h) Introduction

(i) Text (chapters, sections, parts)

(j) Appendixes

(k) Notes

(l) Glossary

(m)Bibliography

(n) Index

A detailed discussion of each of these components is beyond the scope of this book, but there are many good books available devoted to this subject. For starters, you may want to look at *The Chicago Manual of Style*. It has a helpful section on the parts of a book. Indexes are discussed in section **f.** below.

(b) Organizing your book

The table of contents will be structured from your working outline. Now is the time to edit that outline, filling in any blanks and rearranging it to ensure your material flows smoothly and logically. Ensure that recipes are well organized within the chapters, and the chapters well organized within sections (e.g., chapters on fish, poultry, and meat in the entrée section), depending on the extent to which you have subdivided the contents. You may want to review the discussion in chapter 3 about the table of contents.

Proofread your recipes!

Check for:

- Spelling
- Grammar
- Punctuation
- Capital letters
- Abbreviations

The purpose of organizing your book is to make the information in it accessible to readers. In a structural edit, you want to check the organization of your book to make sure you've followed your outline and to ensure the information is indeed accessible to readers. Using standard book organizers that readers recognize, such as a table of contents and an index, will make your book easy to use.

A structural edit will also help you see what is needed or in which area you may be lacking recipes. Do you have too many recipes for desserts and not enough for appetizers?

Finally, a structural edit will allow you to reassess your collection of recipes and the concept of your book, and make sure they are in sync. Make any adjustments necessary to bring the collection and concept in line with each other.

(c) Introductions to sections within the book

Now that you know the general format of your book and how recipes will be organized, you will be able to begin writing the introductions to the various sections. The material you gathered during your research will be invaluable here. The length and scope of each introduction will depend on the subject matter and your own personal writing style. Section **c.2.** of chapter 4 and section **d.6.** of chapter 6 discuss recipe introductions; you will want to use more general information for your section introductions. For example, if you're writing a candy cookbook, you might want to discuss the history and development of chocolate or butterscotch, or possibly write a more personal memory of your childhood experiences with fudge or candied apples.

3. Tool kit for self-editing

The editing guidelines in this section will also be useful applied to your food writing.

(a) Bridges

How do you take readers from here to there? Are there vital links in logic missing? Have you taken flights of fancy and left readers behind? Be sure you have provided the bridges that make your writing flow (seemingly) effortlessly.

(b) Specificity test

Are your images sharp and specific? Sift out all that is vague, distorted, unclear, inappropriate, and boring. Your thesaurus might be of use here.

(c) Tone test

Is your tone appropriate to the subject matter? For example, if your book is written for children, have you written in a fun and light-hearted tone? Have you put a positive spin on things?

(d) Who's talking test

Decide which point of view you prefer to speak from ("I," "you," "they," "one") and stick to it faithfully throughout your book. Otherwise it will become confusing for readers.

(e) Truth test

Does your writing ring true? Does each and every image support your whole thesis? Do not presume to speak for anyone but yourself.

(f) Grammar and spelling

Check and banish those dangling participles and mixed metaphors right now. Use a dictionary or your computer spell check (but be careful: computerized spell checks won't catch misspelled words such as "form" when you want to say "from").

(g) Tenses

Don't run readers through a chaotic time warp of past, present, and future tenses. Be consistent.

4. Working with an editor

Writing is subjective. It has to be. It is an internal, meditative, integrating process. Ideally, editing is objective. It is looking at things from the outside; it is an intellectual stepping back. It takes another mind to do it.

If you're writing for a trade publisher (see chapter 8 for more on publishing), your editor will probably work closely with you and guide you along. Don't be afraid to ask for help. If you're publishing your own book, it is essential that you get the material professionally edited. You will not be able to see your own mistakes.

If you can afford to hire an editor, do so. If not, find someone whom you can trust. Writing is a sensitive process. You do not need cruel, cutting comments even if your work in desperately in need of revision.

A good editor makes things better with the least amount of change. A good editor allows the writer to sing through. There is no change for change's sake. A good editor will reshape a manuscript if necessary, help an author direct and focus the writing, fine-tune words and phrases, suggest development and transitions, move a sentence, and make you sound much smarter. Beware of editors who impose their own ideas on you and criticize you unduly. They can confuse your writing.

Once you have incorporated any of the editor's suggestions you consider valid, print out a corrected copy of the book for yourself and for a proofreader. It is important to have someone proofread the material to catch any typographic errors or other glitches. Then incorporate into the manuscript the proofreader's suggestions you consider valid. Only after the editing and proofreading should you submit your manuscript to either a printer or a publisher.

e. *Illustrations*

Illustrations, the visual communication in your book, are the domain of professional artists and book designers. If you are working with a publisher, the publishing company will hire these people and will decide what illustration is appropriate to your book and how much design work the company can afford.

Color photographs are far more expensive to reproduce than black-and-white drawings. Obviously it is ideal to have your book lavishly and beautifully illustrated. It is, however, a rare writer who has any control over this aspect of the publishing process. If you are fortunate enough to be able to communicate both in text and illustrations, include a few drawings, photographs, or paintings with your book proposal and discuss them early in the negotiations with your publisher. It will go into the early costing of the book.

If you are self-publishing, discuss your options with your printer. Do you have drawings or beautiful photographs? The invention of digital scanners has drastically lowered the cost of printing, even in color.

Food photography is an art involving not only the photographer but also a professional food stylist who sets up the food and props for the shoot. You may wish to hire these professionals to enhance your work.

f. Writing an index

If you want your book to be really useful, it will need an index written by you or by someone commissioned by you or your publisher.

While the table of contents at the beginning of a book is a logical place to look for a certain type of recipe (i.e., appetizer, poultry dish), it is too general to help readers find a specific recipe. The table of contents will refer readers to the first page of a chapter; they would then have the chore of leafing through 30 pages to find the recipe they are looking for. The index at the back of the book is far more detailed.

1. Indexing recipes

Creating an index for your book is part logic, part intuition. The main thing to keep in mind is, "How will readers look something up? How will they use the index?" Readers might remember a fragment of information about a recipe, for example —

- the main ingredient,
- the exact title,
- a few words from the title, or
- the name of the restaurant where the recipe originated, mentioned in the introduction to the recipe.

If it is the first time readers are picking up your book, they may be searching in a more general way. For example, by —

- cooking method (e.g., double-boiler cooking),
- type of food (e.g., cookies),
- cooking utensil (e.g., earthenware),
- ingredient (e.g., duck), or
- general subject (e.g., ecological awareness).

The simplest way to index recipes is to list —

(a) title,

(b) ingredient, and

(c) general subject.

Readers may remember the name of a pie recipe (Gramma's Apple Raisin Pie) or may have a bag of apples (ingredient) and be looking for a way to prepare it, or they may be searching for a new pie recipe (subject). Taking these considerations into account, Sample

If you want your book
to be really useful, it will
need an index.

#13 shows entries under which you might list Gramma's Apple Raisin Pie — the title, subject, ingredients, and an alternate title: apple raisin pie.

If listed by ingredients, recipes are usually listed under the main ingredients. In this example that means under apples and raisins. The number of ingredients you index will depend on how much detail you wish to give and how much space you can allow for your index. Of course, it would not make sense to include every ingredient, such as salt, in every recipe. But whether you wish to include raisins as a subject depends on how important they are to the recipe: does it call for a tablespoon or a cup?

In our example, the subject of the recipe is pie, with a subentry of apple raisin. General subjects for an index are suggested by the logic of the book, which you have outlined in the table of contents. Subjects can be very broad (e.g., pies) or very specific (e.g., deep-dish pies) depending on the focus of your book. If Gramma's Apple Raisin Pie recipe was included in a book about pies, it would be redundant to list it under a general subject ("pie") in the index. However, if it is a deep-dish pie, you may want to enter it under that subentry: deep-dish pie, Gramma's Apple Raisin Pie.

Once you have established a subject heading you will index under, write it down in a list that can be sorted alphabetically by your computer's word processing program, or on cards that can be quickly sorted into alphabetical order. You will want to refer to the list to see what terms you have already used. Using terms consistently is most important.

You would use this same process described above for indexing your book's nonrecipe text. Choose several books that you admire and model your index after theirs.

2. Cross references (see, and see also)

Very few subjects are clear-cut; there are always gray areas. A mechanism for dealing with this is the use of the terms of referral, or cross references. For example:

Cupcakes see Cakes

Crustaceans see Shellfish

Nuts, see also individual names

Custard, see also Puddings

The term "see" is used to guide readers to key terms used, while the term "see also" is used to guide readers to related terms, for additional information.

Be sure to check every single cross reference you create to make sure that the reference exists and that the reference is not blind or circular. Nothing will be more frustrating to readers than to be referred from Crustaceans to Shellfish, and then under Shellfish, back to Crustaceans.

3. When do you write your index?

Although you won't be able to insert the page numbers until you have your cookbook laid out in its final page format (including the finalized page numbers), you can work on your index ahead of time by listing the recipes, ingredients, and other elements that will make up the index. When you have the final pages, you can fill in the page numbers and generally edit the index. The finalization of the index will thus be done right at the end of the prepress stage, so be sure to schedule time for it.

PART III
The Yield

8
Getting your book published

Lots of people dream of opening a restaurant, or writing a cookbook. What stops them? The cold hard business facts, more often than not. It's hard to sustain a dream when the process becomes intimidating and complicated, both technically and financially.

If you are going to get past the fantasy stage, you must believe very strongly in your project. And you have to do your homework. It's one thing to give copies of your favorite recipes to friends who ask for them after a satisfying meal. It's another to go public with them. To publish means to place before the public; to produce or release for publication; to print.

Once you decide to share your culinary skill beyond your kitchen door, you have three options:
- Trade publishing
- Self-publishing using a printer
- Self-publishing on a micro scale, doing it all yourself

113

a. The dollars and cents of publishing

One important factor in your decision to self-publish or approach a trade publisher is money. If you're self-published, you're earning a larger percentage of the retail price of each copy you sell than if your book is trade published. If you sell your books out of the trunk of your car, you earn the difference between your costs and the retail selling price — about 40% to 60%.

Compare this to a good contract with a trade publisher which seldom offers the writer more than 10% of the retail price. However, when your manuscript is accepted for publication by a trade publisher, you will not have any financial obligations — a larger publishing house may even give you a cash advance against future royalties on sales of your book. Also remember that now it is the publisher's obligation to pay for the editing, production, printing, distribution, and sale of your book (unless, of course, your contract says otherwise).

Which option you choose depends on you — your objectives and goals and how much time you are willing or able to put into the project. Both options can prove to be satisfying experiences.

There are many books available that are devoted solely to self-publishing or finding a trade publisher. It may be worth your time to research this more, and talk to writers who have self-published, as well as those who have published with trade publishers.

Later in this chapter you will have a chance to evaluate the number of copies you want to print as well as evaluate your finances. Doing so will help you determine if you can afford to self-publish.

A note about community cookbooks: occasionally charity cookbooks are published by trade publishers who will also handle the marketing of the book. For example, an organization raising money and awareness about legal issues cooperated with a trade publisher in Toronto in a project which involved food writers contributing their favorite recipes to support the cause. Also, the copyright to excellent best-selling community cookbooks are occasionally bought by a trade publisher which brings out a new edition of the cookbook with newer designs and wider distribution.

b. Selling yourself as well as your ideas: the biography

Whether you are going to seek a publisher for your cookbook or have decided to self-publish, you are going to need a biography. A short catchy bio can be used over and over. Material from it can be used on the back cover of your book, in the publisher's or distributor's catalogs, and in press releases. As well, if you are approaching publishers, you'll need a bio for your book proposal package.

A short catchy bio can be used over and over.

If you are looking for a publisher, your credentials and credibility will be important just to get your manuscript looked at. Readers are probably more impressed, for example, by a doctor who writes a cookbook for cancer patients than by a computer programmer who does so. But a home economist who is also a cancer patient may be just as credible as the doctor, or even more so. Think carefully about your credentials and use them to your full advantage — and that of your book.

Take the information you have gleaned from Worksheet #1 and write a lively two-paragraph biography about yourself. Sample #14 is an example of a good short biography. For more examples look at the "about the author" section found in many books.

c. Trade publishers

It's a scary thing: approaching a complete stranger with your heart on your sleeve. Okay, that may sound a bit melodramatic. But the truth is that you have worked for months, even years, nurturing a fragile notion. You've talked to your friends and family about it and researched your topic thoroughly. You've committed it to words on the screen and paper. You may have expended energy in grocery stores, in the kitchen, and at the computer recording and revising your results. You've had total control over your project up to this point.

Some people choose to retain that control by self-publishing. If you decide to go the self-publishing route, you have your own guarantee that you will be in print.

But if part of your plan, or even dream, is to see a title page with both your name and a trade publisher's imprint on it, then you'll need to approach a publisher.

Jacqueline Ehlert, Director of Food Services at Vancouver Community College, brings natural enthusiasm to what is usually considered a rather staid profession. Not content to stay put behind her desk, she can be found cheering on the Canadian Culinary Olympic team, promoting vitamins on CBC Radio's noon show, and teaching night classes to athletes who want to improve their performances through diet.

As an undergraduate at the University of Toronto, Jackie did not merely study her profession — she led the "Wine and Gourmet Society" and developed a low calorie "creamy kiwi ice milk" which she sold to a leading sweetener company.

After graduating with a BA (food/nutrition) she interned at Mount Sinai Hospital and received a Registered Dietitian designation. She worked at Mount Sinai (Toronto) and St. Paul's (Vancouver) hospitals before taking up her present position at VCC.

As a food professional, Jackie feels a deep sense of responsibility to promote healthy eating to the public. She lives her philosophy in her teaching, writing, and speaking, and in her energetic commitment to several industry and educational organizations, including both Canadian and American College and University Food Services Associations, the Canadian Dietetic Association, and Cuisine Canada.

Printed with the permission of Jacqueline Ehlert.

It's more straightforward than you might think. The publisher has a space to fill and you may just be the one to fill it. You have your product and the publisher has a publishing program with goals and parameters. Is there a fit? It comes down to good business on the sides of both partners. A rejection doesn't mean you have a lousy book, just that your square book doesn't fit into their round book list.

If you are a newcomer to writing and publishing, you may find it hard to get the attention of a big city publisher unless you have a dynamite idea and dynamite credentials communicated in a dynamite book proposal. But maybe you don't need a big city publisher. If your book is a combination of local history and recipes, a small local publisher might be a better match for it.

A trade publisher's print run for your book will vary depending on factors such as your book's subject and market, the competition, the size of the publisher, and the production costs of the book. Don't be afraid to ask publishers what their average print runs for books similar to yours are, before you sign a contract.

1. Where do you start?

You have decided you want to approach publishers rather than self-publish. But where do you start?

Look to the title page or copyright page of your favorite cookbooks to find the names of the books' publishers. Check out the new cookbooks on the bookstore shelves. Which books impress you with their professionalism and design?

Back in chapter 1 you researched your competition and noted which publishers are involved in the type of cookbooks you like. You noted which publishers of cookbooks are prominently displayed in the bookstores you visited. You noted whether they are local, Canadian, or American, and whether they are involved in series publishing. Evaluate now if your cookbook idea works with their publishing programs.

Looking for the address of a publisher? Try the reference section of the public library. There are three resources worth looking at:

(a) *Books in Print*. A great resource for a listing of publishers.

(b) *Writer's Market*. This too is a great resource. It lists publishers, the kinds of material they publish, and what they are looking for writers to submit. It also includes contact names and addresses, and tips from editors. Published annually, it has an excellent essay on publishing trends that will fill you in on up-to-date readers' tastes and what other writers are doing to satisfy them. Other essays are included to inspire beginner writers.

(c) *Canadian Writer's Market.* This resource provides up-to-date listings of book publishers and information on the kinds of books they publish, as well as information on magazines, agents, and grants, and other useful advice for writers.

Writers like to write books about writing and there are hundreds of titles on every imaginable topic from writing book proposals to self-publishing to desktop publishing. Many of these topics are dealt with only briefly in this book, so you are well advised to seek out more information in these books found on library shelves. See the Bibliography for information on the books mentioned here and others of interest to writers.

2. The book proposal

A book proposal is the standard way to approach a publisher. It consists of an outline and a description of the book you propose to write, along with other bits of interesting information such as the proposed audience for the book and its competition. Your book proposal must be concise and effective; editors receive many proposals and have only so much time to look at them. The proposal is a true test of your writing skills.

A standard cookbook proposal includes —

(a) a cover letter (also known as a business letter or query letter),

(b) a summary of the general concept (why this book at this time?),

(c) a market analysis,

(d) a brief biography,

(e) a table of contents or chapter outline,

(f) recipe samples, and

(g) writing samples.

Sample #15 shows a sample book proposal for this book.

(a) Cover letter

Length: 1 page

The cover letter is a short introduction to the material you have included with your proposal. Make it short; editors are overwhelmed with mountains of paper. Speak succinctly in a one-page,

How to Write a Cookbook

Have you always wanted to write a cookbook?

Do you have an terrific idea for:

A best-seller?

A self-publishing project?

A limited edition family heirloom?

A community fund-raiser?

This book will take you step by step through the process of creating your own cookbook: how to develop a concept and a table of contents, how to collect recipes and write them out in a professional style, how to interview people, and how to put it all together into your own one-of-a-kind book.

About the author

Judith Comfort has written five cookbooks and is a regular contributor to *Canadian Living* magazine. She teaches a course called "How to Write a Cookbook" at Langara College in Vancouver, B.C., and other courses in food and travel journalism.

Page 1 of 3

Table of contents

1. DEVELOPING A CONCEPT
   - Doing your homework, market analysis

2. COLLECTING RECIPES
   - What to include, research tips

3. TESTING RECIPES
   - Checklist: setting up your test kitchen
   - Standard recipe style worksheet

4. WRITING INTRODUCTIONS TO RECIPES
   - Collecting food memories: where to find them
   - Interviewing tips: checklist of questions to ask

5. PUTTING IT ALL TOGETHER
   - Organizing material
   - Table of contents, indexing

6. PUBLISHING OPTIONS
   - Trade publishers, self-publishing

7. PREPARING A PROFESSIONAL BOOK PROPOSAL
   - Cover letter, your background
   - Detailed outline
   - Sample chapter, tested recipes

8. SELF-PUBLISHING OPTIONS
   - Mass production, limited edition
   - Self-promotion, marketing, distribution

9. PRINTING OPTIONS
   - Laying out, illustrating your book
   - Desktop publishing or simple paste up
   - Creative photocopying options

10. ORGANIZING/MARKETING TIPS FOR FUND-RAISING COOKBOOKS
   - Sample recipe submission forms
   - Community lists

Why this book at this time?

Last year, glossy cookbooks topped the best-seller lists all over North America. Homegrown cookbooks raised funds for museums and hockey teams, and prized hand-written recipe collections passed from one generation to the next. While the publishing industry is constantly scrambling to anticipate the needs of a fickle public, there is one insatiable and unchanging area of reader loyalty — cookbooks. Why? It's hard to say, but everyone has to eat, and cooking is no longer the domain of the mom of the family. People don't have as much time to cook, but they enjoy reading about cooking just the same. And many of these people would love to write a cookbook themselves. *How to Write a Cookbook* will give them the confidence to try.

Many cookbooks are written but never published, for a variety of reasons. This guidebook will be a tool for preparing a more professional, acceptable product.

Another market for this book...

Over the last ten years as a food writer, I have interviewed hundreds of people about their family culinary traditions. Often they pull out a tattered school scribbler with grandmother's neatly penciled recipe for biscuits or War Cake (a Christmas fruit cake of necessity, made with raisins and little else). Today there is a large middle-aged generation anxious to capture family food traditions that may be lost in a few years.

There are also technological choices undreamed of in the carbon paper/Gestetner age: inexpensive laser-printed pages, crisp scanned photographs, and photocopies that reproduce Grandmother's original pencil script so everyone in the family can have a copy.

And another...

Cookbooks continue to be produced by schools, churches, and community groups as fund-raisers. Each group that takes on the task reinvents the wheel. This guidebook would take them through the process with far less effort.

Page 3 of 3

A standard cookbook proposal includes —

- Cover letter
- General concept
- Market analysis
- Brief biography
- Table of contents
- Recipe samples
- Writing samples

single-spaced letter. Wherever possible address the editor by name, which you can get by telephoning and asking the receptionist.

Start with a strong opening and grab the editor's interest. Describe the structure and contents of your book, mentioning your expertise, training, and publishing background (if any).

(b) General concept

Length: ½ to 1 page

In your summary of the general concept of your book, you talk about your compelling idea. Explain why this book, at this time. Provide an overview of the subject and how it will be developed. Show you have done your research, know the subject matter, have background in it yourself, or have tracked down the resources — facts, anecdotes, persons to be interviewed.

(c) Market analysis

Length: ½ to 1 page

In the market analysis, explain who your proposed audience will be and the way you will reach them. Comment briefly about the competition (1 to 2 lines) and emphasize how your book will be different.

(d) Brief biography

Length: ½ to 1 page

Make this author's information sheet interesting. Include notes about your background and qualifications, or a short résumé. As mentioned earlier, this bio can be used later in the book, in a press kit, or in the publisher's catalog.

(e) Table of contents / chapter outline

Length: 1 to 2 pages

When creating the chapter outline you will submit with your book proposal, write one paragraph for each chapter, describing its content and approach to the subject.

(f) Sample recipes

Send in at least ten sample recipes and make sure that they are tested. Your introductions should be enticing. You may want to check to see what recipe style this publisher has used in other cookbooks and format your recipes in this style.

(g) Writing samples

Ideally you have some photocopies of previously published works, perhaps magazine or newspaper clippings, even a column you wrote for a local newsletter. If you don't, and if this is your first book, send in a sample chapter or two.

3. Perseverance

If you have been turned down by a publisher, seriously consider submitting your proposal immediately to another publisher. The second press may very well be pleased to get it. The first publisher may have had all kinds of reasons for rejection that have nothing to do with the quality of your proposal. The press may be overcommitted or simply not in the market for your subject matter (although you will save yourself a lot of time and frustration if you do your research first and target only those publishers that publish cookbooks and material similar to yours).

Be persistent. Research other publishers to approach. Talk to the editors; ask what they are looking for. Above all, don't get discouraged. Your perseverance will likely pay off.

Once your manuscript is accepted by a publisher for acceptance, a whole new process starts, one that is beyond the scope of this book. Do any of your friends have publishing experience? Ask them for advice, or talk to members of writers' circles or writers' groups. Don't hesitate to consult a lawyer if you are not sure how to negotiate the publisher's contract.

d. Self-publishing

A writer may publish his or her own book rather than publish with a trade publisher for many different reasons:

(a) The manuscript has been rejected by publishers, but the writer still feels confident that the project is worthwhile.

(b) The writer wishes to maintain total control of all aspects of book production, including editorial decisions, production schedule, design, printing, publicity, distribution, and sales.

(c) The writer sees a far greater potential for profit in self-publishing. Remember, though, that there is also an element of risk. And publishing your own book requires money up front long before any money is made. However, a successful

The approach you take to publishing a hand-written and hand-bound book with original illustrations for your family is quite different from the approach you would take to publish a best-seller with a press run of 500,000 copies distributed worldwide.

self-published book can often be sold later to a trade publisher, which may repackage or republish and sell under its imprint.

1. Before you take the plunge

Before you take the plunge into the world of self-publishing, assess your needs and goals. The approach you take to publishing a hand-written and hand-bound book with original illustrations for your family is quite different from the approach you would take to publish a best-seller with a press run of 500,000 copies distributed worldwide.

Before taking the plunge, you need to evaluate your own commitment to the project and do a serious financial analysis. Use Worksheet #10 for this exercise. You will need to evaluate whether you have the skills required to publish your own book. If you don't, do you have the time to learn new skills and to expand your knowledge base by taking courses, learning new computer programs, learning research and interview skills, joining a writers' group, or taking a writing class?

You will also need to determine how involved you want to be in the publishing process. At one end of the self-publishing spectrum you simply hand over a manuscript, along with a sum of money, to a vanity press and the press then delivers boxes of the finished product. At the other end of the spectrum you produce a clean digital file of each page and work hand in hand with a myriad of subcontractors.

Now is also the time to consider carefully your finances. Analyze material and office costs, but also consider your unpaid time spent writing, testing recipes, chasing down research materials, interviewing people and talking to designers, editors, printers, and bookstore owners.

Your costs will also depend on your print run. Do you want to produce your cookbook on a micro scale (under 100 copies), on a small scale (under 2,500 copies), or on a large scale (over 2,500 copies). Your research into your market will help you determine how many books you should print. Review chapter 1 if you need more help on making this decision.

2. Printing

In the last 20 years, the rate of technological change in the printing industry has been absolutely astonishing. But some things stay the

Goals:

What are my personal goals?

- ❑ To make a lot of money
- ❑ To bring my body of knowledge to the public
- ❑ To experience the thrill of having a work in print
- ❑ To honor family traditions, such as passing on grandma's recipes to my children
- ❑ Other _____

Skills:

Do I have the skills/knowledge base to publish my own book?

- ❑ Yes
- ❑ No

If no, do I have the time to learn new skills, to expand my knowledge base?

- ❑ Yes
- ❑ No

Time:

How involved do I want to be? _____

Hours per week to commit to project? _____

How long do I expect project to take? _____

From_____to _____

Financial considerations:

How much of my own money am I willing to invest? _____

How long can I wait for a return on my investment? _____

How many copies of my book do I wish to produce? _____

❑　Micro scale (under 100 copies)

❑　Small scale (under 2,500 copies)

❑　Large scale (over 2,500 copies)

Do I have other financial backers? _____

Consider up-front expenses:

_____ Ingredients for recipe testing

_____ Fees for designers, illustrators, text editors, recipe testers, proofreaders

_____ Printing costs

_____ Office supplies: stationery, stamps, telephone

_____ Promotional package materials

_____ Shipping costs

_____ Travel expenses

_____ Unpaid time

same. Printing is still about putting ink on paper and binding the paper together to make books. There are several printing methods available if you plan to have your cookbook printed professionally. (If you plan to publish your cookbook on a micro scale, you will likely print the page yourself. Section **e.** below discusses this option in more detail.)

(a) *Offset lithography*, the most common and reasonably priced method of printing, is a process in which an inked metal plate makes an impression on a rubber-blanketed cylinder and then the inked impression is transferred to paper. It works on the basic principle that oil and water do not mix.

(b) *Laser printing* uses a laser-read photo transfer method of reproduction.

(c) *Quick copy printing* or photocopying uses xerography technology, a dry process that uses electrostatics.

(d) *Quick printing* uses a small cylinder press and plates created using a photo-electrostatic process which results in a raised image that takes the ink and imprints it directly onto the paper.

As a consumer of printing services, you don't need to know how these processes work unless you are just plain curious.

(a) Questions to ask your printer

Visit your nearest printer and ask questions. Get a quote and then get another quote from a different printer. Cheapest is not always best. If you're not in a burning hurry, you may be able to strike a deal. Rush jobs are bound to cost more, so plan wisely. Here are a few questions you should ask the printer:

(a) Can I see samples of books the shop has printed?

(b) What are my options in:

- Paper
- Covers
- Binding

(c) What are printing costs per unit for:

- 1,000 copies
- 2,000 copies
- 2,500 copies
- 3,000 copies

(d) What are my options for handing in a manuscript or disk? Preferred software?

(e) How can I keep expenses down? Are there any stages of the process that I can I do myself?

(f) How long is your quote valid? (Because the cost of paper fluctuates dramatically, most printers give quotes good for up to 30 days only.)

(g) How long will it take to produce the copies from the time I deliver the manuscript or disk?

The average turnaround time — from the time you hand your manuscript on disk to the printer to the time your books are ready to pick up — is about a month. The actual press time is remarkably short, probably less than a day for most press runs. What takes time is the getting-ready-to-go-to-press stage: making the film, proofing, etc.

(b) Printing costs

Rule of thumb:

1,000 copies is the

break-even point in

printing

Printing costs are usually calculated in terms of cost per unit (cost per book). There are considerable hard costs for services, that is, costs you must pay to make your book ready for the press, which remain the same no matter how many copies you print.

Services that are hard costs include preparing the printing plates, making proofs, and setting up the press. These are costs that are incurred whether you make 100 copies or 100,000 copies. The basic rule of thumb is that a press run of 1,000 copies is the break-even point, or the point where the only difference between the cost of producing one book and 1,000 books is the cost of the paper. After 1,000 copies, the unit price starts to drop dramatically. For example, if the press run is 1,000 copies, the printer may charge $5.00 per copy. But if the press run is for 2,500 copies, the cost per unit could drop to $2.10, or less than half.

(c) Paper options

The printer will have hundreds of paper samples. Make a choice based on cost, of course, but also consider the feel and durability of the paper. How long do you want copies of your book to last? The type of binding you choose will affect your choice of paper. For example, newsprint is not good enough quality paper for color photographs and expensive glossy paper is not necessary for a mass market paperback.

Paper is either uncoated or coated. Uncoated paper is more porous. Coated paper is finished with a matte or gloss finish. Photographs reproduce better on coated paper, but photographs on uncoated paper have a softer tone which you may prefer. The cost may not be radically different, but each type of paper will have a different look and feel, so check samples to see what you like. It might be wise to use coated paper for a cookbook susceptible to cooking splashes and greasy fingers.

(d) Paper sizes

Paper used by printers comes in large mother sheets from the mill in various sizes and weights. Bundles of 500 sheets are called reams.

Cutting the paper evenly in such a way as to avoid waste cuts down on your expenses, so consider standard page sizes before getting your heart set on an oddball size.

Mother sheets come in two sizes: 25" x 38" and 23" x 35". Standard size pages efficiently cut from mother sheets are —

- 5.5" x 8.5"
- 6" x 9"
- 8.5" x 11"
- 9" x 12"

(e) Paper weight

Paper is available in different weights based on 500-sheet bundles. Heavier paper is not necessarily thicker. Heavier paper may be sturdier and more aesthetically pleasing, but consider that your books, neatly stored in boxes, will have to be carried from the printer to the car or shipped halfway around the world. As well, you will be paying the shipping costs, which are calculated largely by weight.

(f) Number of pages

Pages of books are printed in what is referred to as *signatures*. A signature is a sheet of paper after it has been folded, resulting in multiples of 4, 8, or, most often, 16 pages. The most cost-effective page count for your book is one that is a multiple of 16. Because the pages within a signature are printed on both sides, you cannot simply add an extra page to your book; the minimum would be a 4-page signature. If you want to add 1 page, you may have blank pages at the end of your book.

Understanding how signatures work will allow you to economize in your printing costs as you will not ask the printer for a custom order with an odd number of pages.

(g) Covers

A color cover is expensive, but without it your book is probably doomed to obscurity. Discuss this topic with your printer at the first meeting. A graphic designer's advice can be invaluable; you may wish to consult one.

You will want your cover to be most attractive from six feet away (it's a little like choosing wallpaper). That's the distance from bookstore shelf to consumers' eyes. A cover should be simple and effective rather than busy. Food photography is extremely difficult for an amateur to do; with an awkward amateurish cover, your book will be judged by — you guessed it — the cover. If you have money to invest in a professional designer and photographer, it will be well worth the effort.

(h) Binding

Binding is the process of collecting and joining single sheets or signatures. There are many binding methods. Which method you choose will depend on the number of pages to be bound, the look you desire, and what you can afford.

(a) *Spiral binding*. With spiral binding, book pages have slotted holes punched or drilled through the gutter (the inside margin) and are held together with plastic coil or spiral wire. The book has no spine, which presents a problem if it is stored in the bookstore, spine out: no title will show. But this type of binding is sturdy and the book opens up flat, which is a distinct advantage for a cookbook. It is possible to add a paper spine to some spiral bindings. Ask your printer.

(b) *Stitching or stapling*. Using the stitching or stapling method, the pages are bound together with staples. There are two kinds: saddle stitching and side stitching.

Saddle stitching is a simple, inexpensive binding that nests the signatures one on top of the other. Two or more staples are then driven through the spine and cover of the book. Magazines are often bound this way.

With side stitching, often used in thicker publications, the staple is driven through the signature from top to bottom.

(c) *Perfect binding*. Perfect binding holds the book together with flexible adhesive glue. The cover is paper and glued on as well. For extra durability, the signatures are sewn together. Most trade paperback books are bound using this method.

(d) *Case binding*. Hardcover books are case bound. This binding is the traditional method of binding books and is far more expensive than the other methods because it involves more steps and materials: sewing, trimming, gluing, lining, covering, casing, applying pressure, and drying.

(i) Keeping expenses down

There are two major things you can do to keep your expenses down when self-publishing:

(a) Keep your manuscript as simple as possible — mostly straightforward text. Graphs, tables, and photographs add to the cost.

(b) Give the printer your manuscript written and formatted. Use any word processing program you like as long as it can be used with a desktop publishing program such as Pagemaker or QuarkXPress. If the printer has to lay out the text, it will pass the cost on to you.

3. Preparing your manuscript for the printer

Giving a printer a hardcopy manuscript is a thing of the past. If you don't have a computer, find someone to input your manuscript onto disk. Your printer may offer the service of typesetting your paper manuscript for you, but you can probably find someone to do it more cheaply.

Most printers require a disk (a digital file) of your manuscript and a black-and-white paper printout of every page. They will need to know which platform you were working in (Mac or PC) and which software you used (Word, Word Perfect, Quark, etc.). Also let them know which version you used.

(a) Desktop publishing programs

Desktop publishing programs are getting easier to use all the time. Given a blank page, the tools to design it, and several hours to learn the program, you can make layout decisions about such things as page size, type (font), illustrations, and margin size. For help in designing your pages, study samples of printing and apply the qualities you like to your own book. Consult books on desktop publishing or consult a professional graphic designer.

If you have limited experience, you may want to take a course in page layout. Many local colleges offer these courses as part of their continuing studies program.

Here are a few simple book design ideas to help you get started:

- Choose fonts, font sizes, and layout that make your text easy to read and compliment the content of the book.

- Lay out the pages so that readers' eyes don't have to skip all over the page trying to find an item.

- Try not to run a recipe over to a second page. (Don't you just hate turning the page to finish a recipe when your hands are covered in flour?)

- Use headings that help readers.

(b) Preferred software

Originally, the standard software for the graphic industry was Macintosh based. Today printers are equipped to handle material from both Macintosh and PC systems. However, always check software compatibility with the printer before committing yourself to a contract. If you are using a program with color, take note that the industry standard is CMYK (Cyan Magenta Yellow Black). If you use RGB (Red Green Blue), you may incur costs to convert it to CMYK. Again, a local course will teach you what you need to know about color printing, or check the many useful resources available at the library.

4. Bluelines

Bluelines are the final check before the book is printed. It will be expensive to make changes at this point, so don't treat it as a standard proofreading stage.

After the printer processes your manuscript, he or she will ask you to check the bluelines. These are prints of your book pages made on light-sensitive paper after your disk has been converted to film. This is the final check before the book is printed. It will be expensive to make changes at this point, so don't treat it as a standard proofreading stage. Whether you check every word, sentence, and paragraph or just skim the bluelines for broken type and obvious errors is up to you and depends often on your time and how carefully your manuscript was proofread before it was given to the printers. The printer will ask you to sign off for any unnoticed errors or omissions.

e. Self-publishing on a micro scale

Almost anyone can make a book. The invention of desktop publishing, the combination of home computers, scanners, laser printers, and photocopiers, has taken the mystique of publishing out of the hands of professionals.

If your aim is to produce handmade treasures for a few people, consider doing it yourself with the help of desktop publishing technology at home or in a copy shop.

1. Pages

You can afford to laser print each page from your home computer or the local print or photocopy shop if you are publishing on a small scale. Quality photocopies may be adequate for your needs, especially if you wish to include photocopies of handwritten pages.

2. Illustrations

Do you draw? Do you have family photographs you want to include? Pen-and-ink drawings can be photocopied and tipped, tacked, or glued in. Old photographs can be copied, enlarged, and photocopied, or duplicated using traditional darkroom techniques.

Handmade watercolors make lovely additions to a book. Photocopy line drawings on high-quality paper and hand watercolor them.

Consider scanning your illustrations; scanning converts them to digitized information which can be printed by a black-and-white or color laser printer.

3. Binding

There are several inexpensive binding options if you plan to self-publish your book on a micro scale:

- Three-hole punch and rings
- Loose-leaf binder
- Duotang
- Ribbons or string (for a homemade touch)
- Brass grommets
- Stapled binding (use a deep throat stapler)
- Handwritten recipes glued into a bound blank book

4. Covers

If you are publishing on a small scale, you may be able to afford to do something more interesting than a standard mass-produced cover. A leather or fabric cover are just two examples. Also consider using photographs or scanned images.

9
Promoting your cookbook

How you promote your book will depend on the subject of your book, how much time and money you are willing to commit, and the extent of your imagination.

Promotion is an area where self-published writers have an advantage over writers who depend on their publishers to promote their books. While most publishers have staff devoted to promotion, they often cannot afford to expend much time or money on promotion unless the cookbook writer is a star. The newly published writer may spend only a day or two on a prearranged book tour.

Many trade publishers will promote cookbooks by arranging a bookstore signing, followed by an interview with the food editor of the local newspaper. The writer will probably hit every area of the local media — newspapers, radio, and television — in a short outburst, but then the publicity will die down.

Always keep track of your expenses. You may be able to use them as a tax deduction.

But because you, as a self-publisher, have an ongoing desire to keep your book in the spotlight, to keep sales up, you can continue promoting your book as long as you like. Don't forget, though, that you may have to cover your own expenses, and no one is paying you an hourly wage to promote your book. Always keep track of your expenses, which can be considerable if you're traveling, taking time away from paid work, and giving away food! You may be able to deduct these expenses from your income tax.

If you've self-published your book (and even if it's been published by a trade publisher), you can create interesting book events. Use your imagination to discover every possible tie-in to promote your book.

Some writers who sign book contracts with trade publishers add a clause giving them the right to purchase books at bookstore discounts and the right to sell their own books. This is the best of both worlds. These writers may earn an advance to offset expenses and can earn more than the standard 10% royalty by selling the books they bought at a discount for the full price. However, if you buy books from the publisher directly, you may lose the royalty on those copies.

A word of caution: be careful where you sell your books yourself. For example, if you sell them in a shopping center, the local bookstore owner will lose those sales and may decide not to stock your book, meaning you may lose an excellent outlet for your books when you're not there to flog them in person.

a. *Where can you sell your cookbook?*

Where should you sell your cookbook? Unlike a writer who is tied to a publisher and a publisher's traditional distribution routes, you can sell your book anywhere, anytime. Keep a few on your person or in the trunk of your car — just in case. Don't make the mistake of assuming that the only place to sell a book is a bookstore. Where have you seen cookbooks?

- Grocery stores
- Gourmet food stores
- Delicatessens
- Drugstores
- Craft shows
- Agricultural fairs

- Gift stores
- School bazaars
- Booths in malls
- Gas stations
- Tourist hot spots: restaurants, motel lobbies
- Museums
- Kitchenware stores
- Cooking schools
- Nightschool classes
- Airports, bus, and train stations
- Convention centers

Approach these venues in person or over the telephone — whatever you feel most comfortable with. Emphasize to the manager of the venue the benefits his or her business could realize by stocking your book. For example, a gas station could use your cookbook as a special promotional item to draw in customers. A cooking class could offer your book as part of the cost of the course, giving students added value for their tuition fees.

Don't ignore the possibility of distributing your books through mail order. There are some excellent books available on operating a direct mail business; check your local bookstore or library, or see *Start and Run a Profitable Mail Order Business*, another book in the Self-Counsel Series.

The idea of direct mail is to target your audience and to send your mailing only to people who might have a genuine interest or need for your book. For example, if you've written a cookbook for diabetics, find out the names of various chapters of diabetic organizations. Send out information on the book along with a mail-order form. Research indexes of organizations to find groups that might be interested in your book.

b. The book launch and book signings

Book launches can be exciting events, comparable to art show openings. They can take the form of a gala dinner launch, featuring chefs and recipes from your book, or a quiet coffee klatch at home.

Choose an exciting theme and entertain people. Serve guests oatcakes and homemade jam prepared from recipes in your Scottish cookbook. Borrow a kilt-clad bagpiper for entertainment. Wear your family tartan. Get as many people involved and create a party. After all, you've really worked hard on your project and you are presenting it to the public for the first time.

Book signings are usually held at bookstores, but they can take place anywhere that people congregate. Have you written a dog-food cookbook? A signing at a dog show or veterinarian's office would be appropriate.

Readers like to meet writers, buy copies of the book for relatives, and ask you to write dedications at the front of the book. Oblige them graciously. Interesting people will come out of the woodwork to discuss the ideas in your book.

Some bookstore owners love to have you come and spice up their store. Enhance your signing by giving away samples of food or by putting on a cooking demonstration.

Sample #16 shows a simple invitation to a book signing that you can model your invitation on.

c. Public events

1. Cooking demonstrations

Cooking demonstrations can take place anywhere: in restaurants and homes, on fishing wharves, on tops of buildings, in cooking classes, at conventions, and in malls. They are a terrific way to be seen and to increase your public image. Don't forget to take boxes of books along to sell on the spot.

Cooking demonstrations are a terrific way to be seen and to increase your public image. Don't forget to take boxes of books along to sell on the spot.

Demonstrations do, however, require a lot of planning. Cooking in a mall may feel like primitive camp cooking, a situation where you can take nothing for granted. Consider the following:

- How will you keep ingredients cool or frozen?
- What surface will you work on?
- Is electricity available? What supplies (e.g., an extension cord) do you need to bring?
- How will you transport materials from your car to the place where you will set up? How many trips will it take?
- Will someone be there to greet you and take care of your parking?
- How will you break camp and clean up?
- How many people are you entertaining?

Sample #16
Invitation to a book signing

ℐnvitation

Attention cookbook lovers . . .

You are cordially invited to meet_____,
author of _____
at _____
at_____ p.m.

The author will be giving away tasty samples of _____
_____,
from her cookbook.

She will be pleased to sign your copy.

- Do you need amplification?

- Are you taking a display?

Contact the person in charge of public relations at the location where your demonstration will be held. This person's help is often invaluable. If he or she cannot help you, ask to be referred to someone who can.

As you plan a demonstration, keep in mind the following tips:

(a) Consider the entertainment value when choosing a recipe for demonstration: does it show off the sounds, sights, and fragrance of cooking? Is it colorful? Are the samples delectable, likely to appeal to many people?

(b) For your own sake, simplify the cooking steps as much as possible.

(c) Prepare as much as possible at home. For example, wash and peel carrots that you will later chop during the demonstration.

(d) Do the samples require knives, forks, plates, and napkins? Have your supplies ready.

(e) Test all your electrical equipment before setting out.

(f) Take lots of garbage bags. You'll use every single one of them.

(g) If you are introducing your demonstration and talking to the audience during cooking, prepare with a dress rehearsal at home, talking into a tape if possible. Watch cooking show hosts and see how they do it.

(h) If possible, take a friend along to the demonstration to help with the setting up, serving, and packing up.

(i) Dress well, but cover yourself with a clean attractive apron.

(j) Don't forget that promotion is the main idea behind the demonstration. Bring along a poster or display on an easel that communicates who you are and what you're selling. A blowup of the cover of your book works well. This is no time to be humble. You can use this publicity tool again and again at bookstore signings and demonstrations, and it will make a wonderful keepsake for your wall.

Use Checklist #3 to ensure you don't forget anything.

Checklist #3
Planning a cooking demonstration

Place: _____

Date: _____

Contact person: _____

Address: _____

Telephone number: _____

Title of dish to be demonstrated (attach recipe): _____

List of ingredients: _____

_____

_____

Generic ingredients to take:
- ❏ Salt and pepper
- ❏ Herbs and spices
- ❏ Water for drinking and washing

Ingredients requiring refrigeration:

_____

_____

_____

Refrigeration method used:
- ❏ Cooler and ice
- ❏ Fridge on premises

Ingredients requiring freezer: _____

_____

_____

Freezing method used:
- ❏ Freezer on premises

Electric kitchen equipment to be taken:
- ❏ Food processor
- ❏ Electric mixer
- ❏ Breadmaker
- ❏ Electric frying pan
- ❏ Wok
- ❏ Electric kettle
  (for heating up water for dishes)
- ❏ Hot plate
- ❏ Hot tray
- ❏ Coffeemaker
- ❏ Heavy duty extension cords

Other: _____

_____

_____

_____

_____

_____

Hand tools:
- ❑ Knives
- ❑ Oven mitts
- ❑ Cutting board
- ❑ Whisk
- ❑ Wooden spoon
- ❑ Cutlery
- ❑ Can opener
- ❑ Vegetable peeler
- ❑ Measuring cups and spoons
- ❑ Matches

Serving materials:
- ❑ Serving platters
- ❑ Trays
- ❑ Paper plates
- ❑ Serviettes/napkins
- ❑ Disposable forks, knives, spoons
- ❑ Disposable cold glasses
- ❑ Disposable hot glasses
- ❑ Disposable wine glasses

Clean-up materials:
- ❑ Dish tubs (for no-sink situations)
- ❑ Plastic bags for garbage and gathering up dirty dishes
- ❑ Paper towels
- ❑ Detergent sprays
- ❑ Dish rags
- ❑ Dish soap
- ❑ Scrubbers
- ❑ Dish towels
- ❑ Plastic wrap or aluminum foil

- ❑ Small food-storage bags
- ❑ Plastic bus tubs for stacking dirty dishes
- ❑ Aprons
- ❑ Latex gloves and Band-Aids

Book promotion materials:
- ❑ Display: sign or poster, book samples
- ❑ Business cards
- ❑ Books to sell
- ❑ Cash box and change
- ❑ Pens for signing books

Large equipment:
- ❑ Table
- ❑ Gauze food covers
- ❑ Podium
- ❑ Microphone and amplifier
- ❑ Cloth backdrop
- ❑ Multiple outlet strip
- ❑ Extension cords

Display items:
- ❑ Basket for displaying ingredients
- ❑ Items for basket: fruit, bread, vegetables
- ❑ Table cloth
- ❑ Fabric drapery
- ❑ Scissors
- ❑ Masking tape
- ❑ Thumbtacks
- ❑ Mirror
- ❑ Camcorder and television monitor

2. Cooking classes

Adult education organizations are always looking for new subjects that appeal to the public. Cookery specialty shops often offer cooking classes. Contact both to offer your services. This is a good way to develop your reputation as an expert in whatever cookery is in vogue. For example, after microwave ovens were introduced to consumers, people flocked to microwave cooking classes. There is also a constant demand for ethnic cooking and nutrition-wise cookery.

3. Speaking engagements

What is the subject of your book? Nursery school food? East Indian family cooking? Cooking for health? There are dozens of organizations and institutions that would enjoy hearing you speak. You've probably already made contact with some of these groups in the course of your research. Church groups and fraternal organizations are also often interested in having speakers. Find out about these groups from friends and colleagues, check the paper for notices, or go to the library and ask for the index of community societies and organizations.

d. Publicity

1. Press releases

A press release disseminates information to the public. Your goal is to publicize your work and sell your book. For example, you have written a collection of recipes for heart-attack patients. The media is looking for information that is newsworthy. What has your research turned up about the connection between heart attacks and diet that would be of interest to the public?

Write your release like a straight news story. Use the journalistic inverted pyramid to tell your story. Ideally, you begin with a lead that will grab editors' attention. There should be enough information in the first sentence or two for editors to quickly decide whether to use your press release or not. The key questions: who, what, when, where, why, and how should be included in this lead. The rest of the information is communicated in order of decreasing importance.

Make your press release as interesting as possible. Quotations add spice. There are many excellent books on writing press releases. Check your local library or bookstore.

Sample #17 shows a sample press release. Your press release should follow the standard format outlined below:

(a) Use plain white paper.

(b) Set margins at one or one-and-a-half inches on all sides.

(c) At top lefthand corner, put your name, address, and telephone number, and the name of a contact person if someone else is setting up interview appointments for you.

(d) At top righthand corner, a few lines down from the bottom of the address, write "FOR IMMEDIATE RELEASE" followed by the date.

(e) At lefthand side, one line below date, write your headline (in capital letters).

(f) Begin the body of the press release one-third down the page, double-spaced.

(g) If two pages are used, place "more" at bottom of the first page.

(h) End release with the word "end" or "30."

Send your press release on its own or as part of a press kit (see section **3.** below) to any media you think might be interested.

2. Review copies

Send review copies to magazines, but be prepared to wait, as much as a year sometimes, before you see anything about your book in print. A magazine may have a lead time of four months, but articles are often assigned a year in advance. Send the editor a press kit (see section **3.** below).

The best promotion for your book would be to give a magazine an excerpt of several pages, including photographs and illustrations, to be printed simultaneously with your book. Readers get a taste of the book in the magazine, then go looking for it in the bookstore. If you plan to do this, you will need to contact the magazine several months before your publication date. Consider how your book concept will coincide with the magazine's publishing program and focus. Is your book relevant to its readers?

Note: If you have trade published, check your contract. Most publishers are licensed to sell these serial rights, giving you a percentage of the royalty. No publisher would complain if you followed up on leads or found avenues for serial rights sales for your book, but you need to be careful how far you go. If in doubt, contact your publisher.

SUSAN SIMON
23 Block Street
Seattle, WA 98225

For interview contact Bill Black:
(360) 555-2345

<u>FOR IMMEDIATE RELEASE</u>
January 23, 199-

BOOK GIVES VEGETARIAN FEASTS AN INTERNATIONAL FLAVOR

If you think vegetarian food means eating boring boiled veggies with rice and beans, think again, says Susan Simon.

In her book *Vegetarian Cooking Goes International*, Simon tells how to prepare healthful vegetarian foods, including high-protein soya products, in a variety of exotic cooking styles. Readers will have fun creating theme meals, while discovering new foods and flavors.

"One day you can try Mexican, the next day Greek or Middle-Eastern," says Simon, whose favorite is Japanese cuisine. "Most of the dishes in my book look fancy, but they are easy on your purse and surprisingly easy to prepare."

The book emphasizes proper nutrition and provides tips for those starting on less-meat and low-calorie diets. Simon uses eggs and milk in her recipes, but suggests alternatives for people on more restrictive diets. Handy meal planning charts recommend food combinations. Here's a sample menu:

Appetizer: Salad rolls, Tom Yum (spicy Thai soup)

Main course: Tofu nuggets with Thai noodles

Side dish: Mixed vegetable curry in coconut sauce

Dessert: Fried bananas drizzled with chocolate

Vegetarian Cooking Goes International will be available March 199- from Green Kitchen Press.

- 30 -

ISBN 0-95459-503-4
$11.95 CAN $9.95 USA
6 x 9, 90 pages, paperback

Printed with permission of Elizabeth Rains.

3. Press kits

Send press kits featuring a press release and a promotional copy of your cookbook to media outlets: radio, television, and newspapers.

Press kits (also called media or information kits) are produced by all kinds of businesses and organizations to get information out to the public. Send press kits featuring a press release and a promotional copy of your cookbook to media outlets: radio, television, and newspapers. When deciding what to include in your release, consider the needs of the people who are receiving the kit. They want to be able to easily extract information from your written work and reconfigure it into their own format. Except in the case of small newspapers hungry for copy, the media will rarely use your material as is.

The use of press releases is a give-and-take situation. The media does you a favor by giving you free publicity. Consider how much it would cost to buy a one-minute spot on radio or television or, alternatively, how much it would cost you in paper, printing, and stamps to reach 2,000 potential book buyers. Fifteen minutes on a call-in show and you reach hundreds, even thousands, of listeners turning on their favorite show.

In return, you must give the editors and producers something of value. You must provide them with content that will please their readers and listeners. Filling space and time is their job. You're in a good position to help because you have probably just completed your research, testing, and writing on a topic about which you are now knowledgeable, even impassioned. Your aim is not only to explore the topic but also to tantalize listeners or readers into buying your book. Your press kit should sincerely show the media what it is you have to offer. It could be a fascinating point of view, even some controversy. Entertainment is part of your mandate.

The basic contents of a simple press kit are —

(a) a cover letter listing the contents of the kit,

(b) a copy of the cookbook (this is the most important component),

(c) a press release, and various options including —

(d) a brief biography of the author, especially if you have impressive credentials, and a photograph, *or*

(e) a backgrounder if there are lots of interesting facts a reporter can use to fill out the story, *or*

(f) questions and answers about the book, *or*

(g) a gimmick that suits the theme of your book. For example, a bookmark with a gingerbread recipe, printed on brown stock and cut in the shape of a cookie dough man, could promote a Christmas cookbook. If you're daring, you might even include the cookie, assuming it is packaged well.

What gimmicks you include depend, in part, on your budget. Some ideas are a poster of the book cover, coupon to a dinner launch, raffle ticket, T-shirt, balloon, or postcard.

Package your press kit in the most appropriate, attractive folder you can afford.

4. Radio and television station contacts

Do your market research by monitoring each station carefully to discern which shows might grant an interview to a cookbook writer. Consider local, regional, and national stations. Don't forget stations in other cities that reach a local audience. Do you have an angle of particular interest to them? You can get a list of contacts from an almanac in the reference section of the public library. Identify the contact person by calling the general business number and asking the receptionist to whom you should send the press kit. Be prepared to be put through immediately. You may get an opportunity to book a time to tape an interview on the spot. Use Worksheet #11 to track the different stations you research.

5. Print contacts: newspapers, magazines, and newsletters

Scan local, regional, and national newspapers, especially ones that have food sections. What kind of coverage do they give to cookbook writers? Will they likely review your book or interview you, the author? Contact the food editor where possible. Does your book have a local connection, perhaps including historical research and the names of many local residents? If you live in a rural area, the local paper may want to interview you as a local celebrity.

Contact the food editors of magazines by mail or by phone. Send a press kit, including a review copy of your book. Sell your submission as something absolutely new or different that cannot be duplicated by staff or the editor's regular freelance writers. Be open to an editor's suggestions. Many are sympathetic and helpful. Perhaps they will suggest a different way of using your material or will ask that you write a freelance article for them, perhaps on a completely different topic.

Radio/television station: _____

Name of show: _____
_____

Time aired: _____
_____

Producer/contact person: _____
_____

Telephone: _____
Optimum time to call (non-airtime): _____

Host: _____

Theme: _____
_____

Audience: _____
_____

Other notes: _____
_____
_____
_____
_____

If your book concept appeals to a niche market (e.g., a dehydrated, lightweight food cookbook), consider sending promotional copies to relevant associations (e.g., a backpacking association). You can find a list of societies and associations at the library. Look beyond your local organization; when you're doing mail order, for example, your market is the world.

Call the organization to see if it has a newsletter. Search the Internet to see if it has a Web site. You may want to consider writing a free article for the organization's print or on-line newsletter, including your contact name and address at the end of it. You may also want to consider purchasing a small advertisement, especially if you are selling your book through the mail. Worksheet #12 will help you track appropriate print contacts.

Look beyond your local organization; when you're doing mail order, for example, your market is the world.

e. Other ideas

1. Gimmicks and gift packs

Gimmicks work! Give away postcards, bookmarks, recipe cards, posters, balloons, T-shirts, or buttons. Hold contests. Why not? — they're fun! Put a contest form for a prize draw right in your book at the point of sale. Combine some of these activities with appearances in bookstores or trips to schools.

Combine books and merchandise in a gift pack, depending on the theme of your book. For example, include a tiny package of exotic rice with a rice cookbook. Or attach a disposable bib to a baby-food cookbook.

2. Paid advertisements

Paid advertisements in newspapers, trade publications, and general interest magazines may or may not be a good value. Consider the shelf life of your ad. A tasteful ad in the back of a well-known and respected magazine will be on the store shelves for a month and on people's coffee tables for months or even years. Your ad in the local paper is considerably cheaper, but it is also on its way to recycling the next day.

3. The Internet

Many books are now promoted on the Internet. Find a company that offers the service of putting your book on-line. The typical method of grabbing readers' attention is to publish a few pages or even a chapter of the book, which people can read and download for free.

Worksheet #12
Newspaper and magazine contact list

Newspaper/magazine title: _____

Address: _____

_____

Telephone: _____

E-mail:_____

Food editor or contact person: _____

Book review section: ❑ yes ❑ no

Features interviews with cookbook authors: ❑ yes ❑ no

Readership profile: _____

_____

_____

_____

Other notes: _____

_____

_____

_____

_____

_____

You hope it will pique their interest so they will want to purchase the whole book. You can sell them the book electronically (mail it to them by e-mail) or arrange to have the paperbound book delivered the old-fashioned way, to the door.

4. Form a partnership

Form a partnership with a commercial company. Help that company promote its product by showing consumers how to use it in dozens of ways (for example: bread machines in a baking cookbook, soy sauce in a cookbook on Chinese cookery). The company promotes your book by featuring it in its advertisements or giving it away with its product.

Marketing boards that promote agricultural products may allow you to set up your book stand next to their booth at trade shows and exhibitions. Know a million ways to cook seaweed? To finance and promote your book, find a fisheries department that is developing consumer taste in "ocean vegetables." Or contact an egg council, potato marketing board, or apple growers association if you've got an egg, potato, or apple cookbook.

5. Newsletters

Start a newsletter for your readers. Create a loyal following of readers who will recommend your book to their friends and buy your next release.

Form a partnership with a commercial company: you promote the company, the company promotes you.

A brief afterword...

The purpose of this book is to give you the tools to fulfill your dream of writing a cookbook. Where you lack confidence I hope to provide you with a starting point. I hope, even, to inspire you. I'd love to hear success stories. Please drop me a note addressed to my publisher.

What if you've come this far and feel discouraged? Go back to the first chapter and re-read what is written about ideas. So what if you've done your research and decide your idea won't fly. Grab another one out of the air! If you feel that it's really not for you, that's fine too. Perusing the bookstore display of new cookbook titles, you'll now appreciate how much work went into them. But don't throw your notes in the garbage. Who knows, maybe next year you'll feel energized enough to start all over again. Take care, and best of luck.

Appendix 1:
Cooking terms

a. Terms of food preparation and process

It is important to understand the terms you use and to use them consistently.

Bard
To cover meat with a thin layer of fat

Bread
To coat with bread crumbs

Brush
To coat lightly with liquid using a pastry brush

Chill
To refrigerate food or stand over ice until cold

Cool
To allow mixture to come to room temperature

Cure
To preserve meat by a combination of drying, salting, smoking

Dissolve
To make a solution, to melt or liquefy

Dot
To scatter bits of fat over surface of food

Dredge
To cover solid food with dry powdery ingredients such as flour, sugar, bread crumbs, cornmeal, or similar substances

Drizzle
To lightly sprinkle drops of liquid over food

Dust
To sprinkle food with dry ingredients such as flour or icing sugar

Flambé
To ignite warmed alcoholic beverages over food

Flute
To make decorative indentations, scalloped, or undulating edges on pastry

Garnish
To decorate

Glaze
To coat with a semiliquid glossy mixture

Knead
To work dough with hands or machine to develop gluten in flour

Lard
To insert strips of fat called lardoons into lean meat to tenderize, give texture, or add flavor

Marinate
To tenderize and flavor foods by covering in seasoned, acidic liquid

Mold
To form food into a shape by filling a mold or decorative container followed by steaming, chilling, baking, or freezing, and finally removing or unmolding on a platter

Pickle
To preserve in salt brine

Pipe
To squeeze a soft mixture through a pastry bag or tube to make a decorative shape or trim

Proof
To test the activeness of yeast

Punch down
To deflate a yeast dough by pushing down on it

Reconstitute
To add water to concentrated foods such as powdered milk and frozen fruit juice

Roll out
To flatten, using a rolling pin, to the required shape and thickness

Truss
To tie poultry with string so that it will keep its shape during cooking

b. Stovetop cooking terms

Blanch

To immerse foods in boiling water for an instant, often followed by quick cooling in cold water

Boil

To heat liquid until bubbles rapidly break out on the surface

Braise

To cook food slowly in a small amount of liquid or fat in a covered pan on the stovetop or in the oven

Brown

To sear food, usually in a small amount of fat, to seal in juices until it darkens

Caramelize

To heat sugar, or sugary foods, in a skillet over low heat until it turns brown and develops caramel flavor

Clarify

To separate solids from a liquid, making it clear (e.g., butter, stock)

Coddle

To simmer gently in water just below the boiling point

Cook

To prepare food for eating by means of heat

Deep-fry

To cook food in hot fat that is deep enough for the food to float

Deglaze

To make a natural sauce using the glaze from a pan in which meat, fish, or poultry is cooked. Liquid is added to dissolve the particles; this may be cooked down to a more concentrated form or butter may be added

Degrease

To remove fat from soup, gravy, or sauce by skimming liquid or by chilling and removing solid fat

Fricassee

To stew gently in liquid with vegetables

Fry

To cook in a skillet with fat

Parboil
To precook in boiling water, similar to blanching

Poach
To cook in simmering liquid

Reduce
To boil down to decrease the volume

Render
To melt solid fat to a liquid state by heating it (also in oven)

Sauté
To fry gently in a skillet with less fat and over lower heat than frying

Scald
To place food in boiling water and remove it immediately or to bring milk just to a boil

Sear
To brown surfaces of meat quickly to seal in juices

Simmer
To cook gently just below the boiling point so that bubbles barely form on the surface

Skim
To remove film or fat from surface of food

Steam
To cook food with steam by placing it over, but not touching, boiling water, either on a rack in a covered pot or sealed in a metal pudding mold

Steep
To pour boiling water over food and allow it to sit in order to extract flavor or color

Stew
To cook food slowly over low heat in liquid (oven also)

Stir
To mix ingredients with a circular motion in a bowl or pan to ensure even cooking and to prevent sticking

Stir fry
To fry sliced foods quickly over high heat in a wok, Chinese-style

c. *Oven cooking terms*

Bake
To cook by dry uncovered heat

Baste
To moisten food while cooking with melted butter, fat, or liquid

Broil
To cook under or over direct heat on a grill or spit

Preheat
To turn on oven ahead of time to ensure that it is sufficiently heated to the desired temperature before adding food

Roast
To cook by dry heat in oven, usually large cuts of meat, not meat combinations or small servings

Sear
To seal juices in meat by placing in oven at very high temperature

Toast
To crisp outside of food by broiling or grilling or in a hot oven

d. *Terms of combination*

Beat
To make a mixture smooth and light by incorporating air with rapid, circular motion, using a fork, whisk, wooden spoon, or electric mixer

Blend
To incorporate two or more ingredients together to form a homogeneous mixture or to process food in a blender

Combine
To stir two or more like ingredients together to form a mixture of uniform consistency

Cream
To make soft and smooth or to blend by beating

Cut in
To distribute shortening into flour or flour mixtures with a pastry blender or two knives until it resembles coarse crumbs

Fold
To gently incorporate a light substance into a heavier one using a rubber spatula or spoon; to retain volume and lighten mixture using a motion of cutting from top to bottom, sliding across the bottom then up again in a circular motion

Mash
To beat into a smooth puree

Mix
To combine two or more ingredients

Rub-in
To rub fat and flour between finger tips until it resembles coarse bread crumbs

Sift together
To combine and lighten dry ingredients by pushing through a sifter

Whip
To beat with mixer or by hand to lighten mixture and increase volume

Whisk
To beat with a whisk

e. Cutting and texture-altering terms

Bone
To remove bones from meat, poultry, or fish

Chop
To cut food into pieces with a knife, blender, or food processor

Cube
To cut into small cubes approximately half an inch (one cm) square

Dice
To cut food into very small even pieces by making even horizontal and vertical cuts

Eviscerate
To remove internal organs of fish or poultry

Fillet
To debone fish or meat

Flake
To break into small pieces, often with a fork

Grate
To break into small pieces by rubbing solid food against a metal or plastic object with sharp-edged holes

Grind
To process solid food with mortar and pestle, food grinder, food processor, or blender to reduce it to particles

Julienne
To cut into long thin strips

Mince
To chop into very fine pieces

Pare
To shave away the skin or rind of fruit

Peel
To remove the peel of vegetables or fruits by hand or with a knife or vegetable peeler

Pit
To remove seed by hand or with a knife or pitter

Puree
To mash to a smooth blend by pressing through a food mill or processing in a blender or food processor

Score
To make shallow cuts in meat or fish to promote tenderness or prevent fat from warping during cooking

Scrape
To remove peel by scraping rather than cutting with a knife or peeler

Shred
To cut or grate into shreds

Sieve
To push food through a sieve to remove lumps or make a puree

Sift
To push through a sifter to remove lumps and lighten ingredient, often flour

Slice
To cut into thin flat pieces or wedge-shaped portions or slices

Sliver
To cut into long thin pieces

Snip
To cut into fine pieces, with scissors

f. Other

Barbecue
To cook on a grill or spit over an intense heat of charcoal, wood fire, or gas-heated coals

Barbecue
To cook in a highly seasoned vinegar sauce

Grill
To cook on a grill over intense heat

Plank
To attach ingredient to a plank of wood and place before an open fire

Appendix 2:
Metric/imperial conversion charts

Note: These measurements are approximations only.

a. Temperature

CELSIUS	FAHRENHEIT	
-18 °C	0 °F	freezer temperature
0 °C	32 °F	freezing point of water
4 °C	40 °F	refrigerator temperature
29 °C	85 °F	yeast dough rises
38 °C	100 °F	lukewarm to touch
43 °C	110 °F	scalding hot
46 °C	115 °F	
57 °C	135 °F	
60 °C	140 °F	
66 °C	150 °F	
71 °C	160 °F	
74 °C	165 °F	
77 °C	170 °F	
82 °C	180 °F	simmering point of water
88 °C	190 °F	
95 °C	200 °F	warming oven
96 °C	205 °F	
100 °C	212 °F	boiling point of water
110 °C	225 °F	
120 °C	250 °F	very slow oven
135 °C	275 °F	
150 °C	300 °F	slow oven
165 °C	325 °F	moderately slow oven
180 °C	350 °F	moderate oven
190 °C	375 °F	moderately hot oven
205 °C	400 °F	hot oven

CELSIUS	FAHRENHEIT	
220 °C	425 °F	
230 °C	450 °F	very hot oven
245 °C	475 °F	
260 °C	500 °F	oven broiling

b. Measure

1. Volume

METRIC	IMPERIAL
1 mL	¼ teaspoon (slightly less)
2 mL	½ teaspoon (slightly less)
5 mL	1 teaspoon
15 mL	1 tablespoon
25 mL	1 tablespoon plus 2 teaspoons
50 mL	¼ cup (slightly less)
75 mL	⅓ cup
100 mL	½ cup (slightly less)
125 mL	½ cup (slightly more)
175 mL	¾ cup
250 mL	1 cup (slightly more)
375 mL	1½ cups
750 mL	3 cups
1 L	4 cups

2. Length

METRIC	IMPERIAL
5 mm	¼ inch
1 cm	½ inch
2 cm	¾ inch
2.5 cm	1 inch
5 cm	2 inches
10 cm	4 inches

3. Weight

METRIC	IMPERIAL
28.4 g (rounded to 25 g)	1 oz.
50 g	2 oz.
125 g	¼ lb.
250 g	½ lb.
454 g (rounded to 500 g)	1 lb. (16 oz.)
1 kg (1,000 g)	2.2 lb.
1.5 kg	3 lb.
2.2 kg (rounded to 2 kg)	5 lb.

c. Utensils

COOKING UTENSIL	METRIC (diameter x depth)	IMPERIAL
Round cake pan	20 x 4 cm	8 x 1.5 inch
Round cake pan	23 x 4 cm	9 x 1.5 inch
Square cake pan	20 x 5 cm	8 x 2 inch
Square cake pan	23 x 5 cm	9 x 2 inch
Pie plate	20 cm	8 x 1.25 inch
Pie plate	23 cm	9 x 1.5 inch
Pie plate	25 cm	10 x 1.75 inch
Loaf/bread pan	20 x 10 x 7 cm	8 x 4 x 3 inch
Loaf/bread pan	23 x 13 x 7 cm	9 x 5 x 3 inch
Casserole	1 L (15 cm)	1 quart (6 inch)
Casserole	2 L (21 cm)	2 quart (8.5 inch)
Casserole	3 L (25 cm)	3 quart (10 inch)
Springform pan	23 cm	9 inch
Springform pan	25 cm	10 inch
Custard cups	150 mL (8 cm)	3 inch
Custard cups	300 mL (11 cm)	4.5 inch

Appendix 3:
Liquid and dry volume equivalents

Note: These equivalents are approximations only.

pinch, few grains, dash	= less than ⅛ teaspoon	
60 drops	= 1 teaspoon	= 5 mL
1 teaspoon	= ⅓ tablespoon	= 5 mL
3 teaspoons	= 1 tablespoon	= 15 mL
2 tablespoons	= 1 fluid ounce	= 25 mL
4 tablespoons	= ¼ cup	= 50 mL
5.3 tablespoons	= ⅓ cup	= 75 mL
8 tablespoons	= ½ cup	= 125 mL
16 tablespoons	= 1 cup	= 250 mL
1 cup	= 8 fluid ounces	= 250 mL

Appendix 4:
Standard terminology in recipe writing

It is important to use consistent vocabulary from recipe to recipe. You will confuse readers if you call something a saucepan on one page and a pot on another, or if you use white flour and all-purpose flour interchangeably. You may even want to define terms. What exactly to you mean by chop, mince, cube?

Following is a list of varied terms. When you have decided which ones you prefer to use, simply place a pencil check mark to the left. Once established, you can refer to your standard vocabulary list to see what term you have used in the past. Feel free to add new terms, as long as readers will be clear what is meant.

a. Instructions

Add	Combine	Flambé
Arrange	Cook	Flute
Bake	Cover	Fold
Barbecue	Cream	Fricassee
Bard	Crimp	Frizzle
Baste	Cube	Fry
Blanch	Cure	Garnish
Boil	Curry	Glaze
Braise	Cut in	Grate
Brew	Deglaze	Griddle
Bring to a boil	Degrease	Grill
Broil	Devil	Grind
Brown	Dice	Heat
Bruise	Dredge	Julienne
Butter	Drizzle	Knead
Caramelize	Drop	Ladle
Chop	Dust	Lard
Clarify	Eviscerate	Marinate
Coat	Fillet	Mask
Coddle	Fire	Measure

Microwave
Mince
Mix
Mold
Oven-bake
Pan
Pan Broil
Parboil
Pare
Peel
Pickle
Pinch
Pipe
Plank
Plump
Poach
Pour
Prepare
Press
Process
Proof
Pulse

Pulverize
Puree
Put
Quarter
Reduce
Refresh
Reheat
Render
Reserve
Roast
Rub
Sauté
Scald
Scallop
Score
Sear
Set Aside
Shirr
Shred
Sift
Simmer
Slice

Soak
Spin a thread
Spoon
Steam
Steep
Stew
Stir
Stir in
Stir-fry
Taste
Temper
Tie
Toast
Toss
Truss
Unmold
Whip
Whisk
Whisk in
Whisk together

b. Cooking utensils/appliances/kitchen equipment

Apple corer
Baking dish
Baking pan
Baking sheet
Bean pot
Blender
Boning knife
Bottle opener
Bowl
Bread knife
Bread machine
Bread pan

Breadbasket
Broiler
Brush
Bulb baster
Bundt pan
Cake pan
Cake rack
Can opener
Candy thermometer
Carafe
Carving knife
Casserole

Cast iron skillet
Caster
Chafing dish
Cherry pitter
Chopping block
Chopping board
Chopsticks
Clay cooker
Coffee cup
Coffee maker
Colander
Compote